CAMBRIDGE INTRODUCTION TO WORLD HISTORY
GENERAL EDITOR · TREVOR CAIRNS

The Growth of a Medieval Town

Lincoln from the Norman Conquest to the Wars of the Roses

Dulcie Duke

CAMBRIDGE
UNIVERSITY PRESS

Front cover: *A fourteenth-century artist's impression of a medieval city. The drawing is supposed to show the city of Constantinople, but the artist was probably basing his picture on the nearest walled city he knew: the city of Lincoln. You can see the cathedral with spire and weathercock, the houses with roofs of thatch or tile, and shop signs hanging outside.*

The picture comes from the 'Luttrell Psalter', a book of psalms which was illustrated by local artists for a Lincolnshire knight, Sir Geoffrey Luttrell, shortly before his death in 1345.

Back cover: *Lincoln Cathedral: a present-day view.*

Drawings by Anna Mieke
and Barry Eyden
Maps by H.A. Shelley and Reg Piggott (p.5)

The author and the publisher gratefully acknowledge the assistance given towards the illustration of this book by the librarian and staffs of the Lincoln City Library, Museum and Art Gallery, the County Archivist, the Subdean and the Chancellor of Lincoln Cathedral, and the Lincoln College of Art.

Thanks are also due to the following for permission to reproduce illustrations in this book:

p. 8 (Bayeux tapestry) Phaidon Press Ltd; pp. 6, 9 (engraving), 18, 20 (seal), 22, 23 (pottery), 29 (coin), 35 (charter), 38, 41, 43, 45 Lincoln City Library, Museum and Art Gallery Department; pp. 7 (charter), 15 (west front), 26 (calendar), the Dean and Chapter, Lincoln Cathedral, photographer M. Young; p. 7 (coins) Sir Francis Hill; pp. 9 (stonework), 24, 25, Lincolnshire Echo; p. 10 (chest) Rev. R. J. Graham, Howden Minster; p. 10 Mike Duffy, York Archaelogical Trust; pp. 11, 12, 13, 15 (bear), 23 (well), 30, 31, 33 (cart and windmill), 36, 37, the Mansell Collection; pp. 14, 26, 27, 31 (detail of an angel) Courtauld Institute; p. 19 (guild warden) British Museum; p. 19 (St Mary's Hall) Lincoln Civic Trust; p. 20 (Magna Carta) S. Harrop; pp. 23 (stonework), 32, 46, 47 Bertl Gaye; p. 35 Ipswich Museums and Art Galleries; p. 39 The Public Record Office; pp. 34, 42 and back cover, The City of Lincoln; p. 44 The Mayor and Corporation of Lincoln City; p. 48 Cambridge University Department of Aerial Photography.

Maps are based on those in Sir F. Hill, *Medieval Lincoln*, Cambridge University Press. The cover picture from the Luttrell Psalter is by courtesy of the Trustees of the British Museum.

Published by the Press Syndicate of the University of Cambridge
The Pitt Building, Trumpington Street, Cambridge CB2 1RP
40 West 20th Street, New York, NY 10011-4211, USA
10 Stamford Road, Oakleigh, Victoria 3166, Australia

© Cambridge University Press 1974, 1988

First published 1974 as *Lincoln: the growth of a medieval town*
Reprinted 1976, 1980, 1983
Second edition 1988 as *The growth of a medieval town*
Reprinted 1989, 1992

Printed in Hong Kong by Wing King Tong

British Library cataloguing in publication data

Duke, Dulcie
    The growth of a medieval town: Lincoln from the Norman Conquest to the Wars of the Roses. – 2nd ed. – (Cambridge introduction to world history).
    1. Lincoln (Lincolnshire) – History
    I. Title   II. Duke, Dulcie. Lincoln, the growth of a medieval town

    942.5′34   DA690.L67

Library of Congress cataloging in publication data

Duke, Dulcie.
    The growth of a medieval town.

(Cambridge introduction to world history)
    Summary: Examines housing, transportation, trade, warfare, and other aspects of medieval life in the English town of Lincoln from the Norman conquest to the Wars of the Roses.
    1. Lincoln (Lincolnshire) – History.   2. Cities and towns, Medieval – England – Lincoln (Lincolnshire) – History. 3. England – Civilization – Medieval period, 1066-1485. [1. Lincoln (Lincolnshire) – History.   2. Cities and towns, medieval – England – Lincoln (Lincolnshire)   3. England – Civilization – Medieval period, 1066-1485] I. Title.   II. Series.
DA690.L67D84   1987   942.5′34   87–6609

ISBN 0 521 33725 9

Contents

Introduction

1 At the time of the Norman Conquest   *page 5*
The Conquest   5
Lincoln   5
The castle   8
The houses in the town   10
Freemen and taxes   12
The Church   14
Leisure time   15

2 In the time of Magna Carta   17
The Jews   17
Guilds   17
The mayor   19
The houses in the town   21
The castle   24
Hugh, Bishop of Lincoln   26

3 From King John to the Black Death   29
Edward III comes to Lincoln   29
Transport   34
The wool Staple   35
Markets and fairs   37
The friars   38
The Black Death   39

4 In the time of the Wars of the Roses   41
The Wars of the Roses   41
The guildhall   43
Hard times   44
Town houses   45

This book is about English towns during the four and a half centuries we call the Middle Ages. It tells the story of one town in particular – Lincoln.

At the time of the Norman Conquest, Lincoln was already one of England's largest towns, with over 5,000 people. London, the capital, had 15,000. Other towns had only a few hundred inhabitants and most of England's population lived in villages rather than towns.

By the time the Black Death arrived, about three hundred years later, more than 140 new towns had grown up. Towns were the homes of merchants and workers who specialised in particular crafts. Trade centred on the market at the heart of each town. Each town had been granted a charter by the king which allowed the people to govern their own affairs. Many towns had walls and gates, a castle, large churches and public halls. In Lincoln, as in many English towns, you can still see today the remains of a rich medieval past.

The story begins in 1066 with the Norman Conquest.

At the time of the Norman Conquest

William I leads his army through Lincoln, 1068

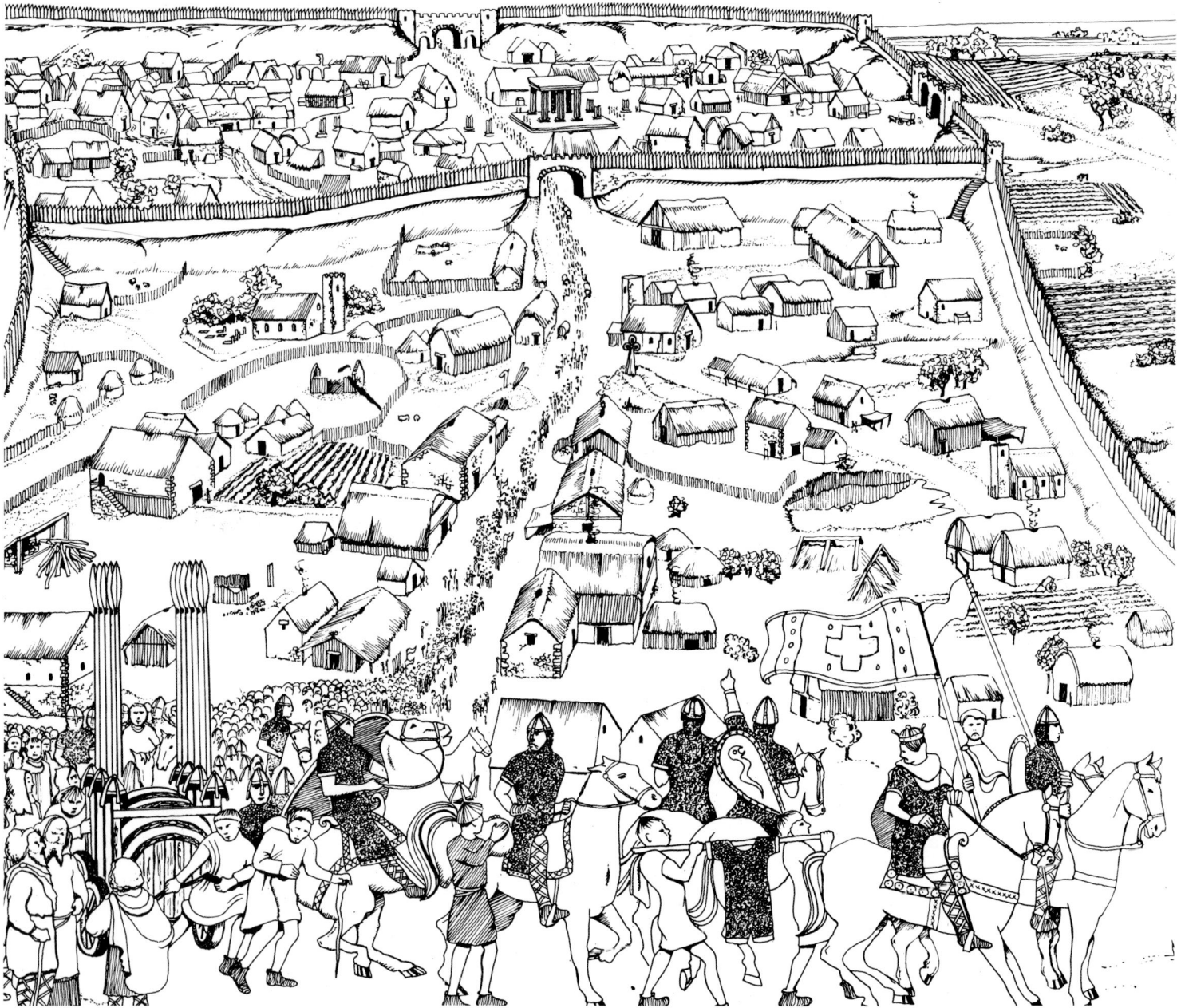

1 At the time of the Norman Conquest

The Conquest

In 1066 England was invaded by a Norman army led by their duke, William. They were opposed by the English king, Harold II, and an English army. In the subsequent battle on Senlac Hill near Hastings the English were defeated and King Harold killed. Duke William of Normandy became King William I of England and was called 'the Conqueror'.

However, people do not easily accept conquest and there were attempts to drive out the Normans by many English who did not want the change. Some of the English leaders turned to Edgar the Aetheling, who they thought had a claim to the English throne. Edgar and his sisters had appealed to Malcolm Canmore, King of the Scots, for help, and had taken refuge at his court. Here they were joined by other English people.

In 1068 the city of Exeter tried to form a resistance group among the neighbouring towns. William marched an army against Exeter, which held out for eighteen days and only surrendered on the understanding that the town would keep all its privileges. William returned from Exeter to London where he held his court and where Mathilda, his wife, was crowned queen of England.

After these ceremonies William journeyed north to York, which he entered without a battle. At York he got the formal submission of many local leaders and arranged a truce with the Scottish king. Then he returned to London by way of Lincoln, Huntingdon and Cambridge.

Medieval towns in England

Large towns (over 5000 people) in Norman times
Large towns around 1380
Towns with Medieval remains; walls, gateways, buildings

Lincoln

From pre-Roman times there has been a settlement on the site of Lincoln – on the limestone ridge where the River Witham bends sharply east towards the sea (see map on page 6, below). From the 'fort by a pool' (or *Lincoln* as the Britons called it), a watch could be kept on the North. There was a danger of attack from invaders coming up the River Humber.

The hill fort was protected to the south and west by marshes, fens and dense woods. Later the Romans named the settlement *Lindum colonia*, and hence its present-day name *Lincoln*.

The picture opposite shows William entering Lincoln, having led his army from the north along the Roman road,

5

Ermine Street. Like many other towns that the Normans occupied when they invaded England, Lincoln had kept its shape since Roman times. At the top of the picture (the north end of Lincoln) you can see the old fortifications which the Romans built, still forming the walls of the town. There are few other traces of the Romans, however. Their streets, sewers and buildings have mostly disappeared.

William was met by the most important people of Lincoln. Most carried on in office after the Conquest and some were rewarded for accepting the new rulers. But there were new Norman leaders as well. One of them was the first bishop of Lincoln, Remigius. He had been prior of the Norman abbey of Fécamp and had persuaded his fellow monks to give William a ship for his invasion of England and to hire knights to fight for him. His contemporaries accused Remigius of ambition. Certainly when the last English bishop of Dorchester on Thames died in 1067 Remigius was appointed in his place. Four years later, in 1071, William ordered Remigius to build a cathedral at Lincoln and to move his bishop's chair from the little town of Dorchester to the larger town of Lincoln.

Newport arch. William probably entered Lincoln through this arch. This is all that remains of the great Roman gatehouse build in the second century AD. The centre arch is 4.8 m (16 ft) wide and was originally 6.7 m (22 ft) high though it is lower now because the road level has risen by 2.4 m (8 ft).

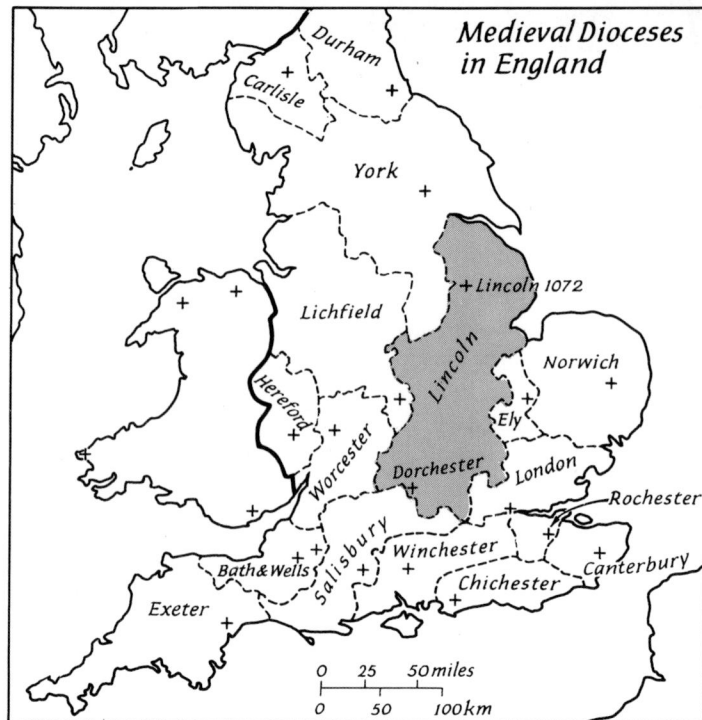

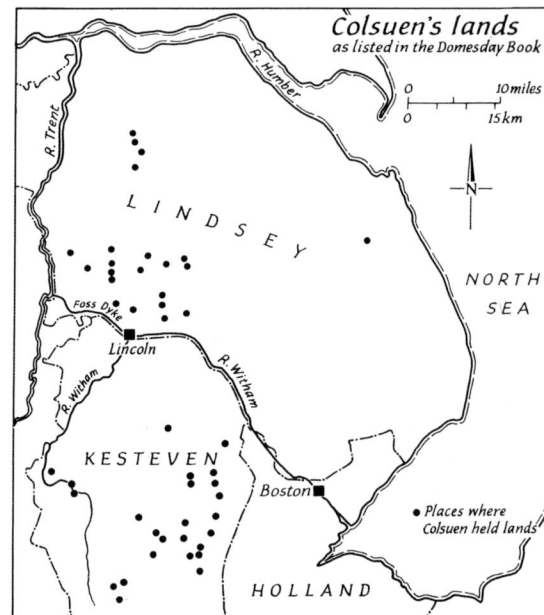

Medieval Dioceses in England

Colsuen's lands as listed in the Domesday Book

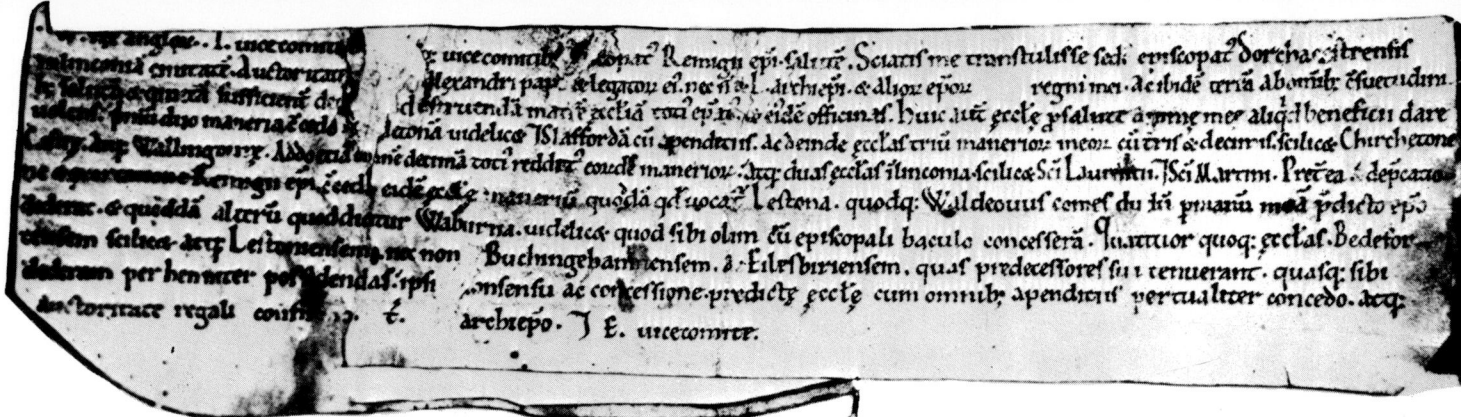

The charter which William issued in 1071 is still kept in Lincoln cathedral. It is written on parchment but not signed. It concludes with the initials of two important witnesses, Lanfranc, archbishop of Canterbury and Ernwiss, the local sheriff. Translated the Latin begins: 'William, king of the English, to Thorold the sheriff and to all the sheriffs of the diocese of Bishop Remigius, greeting. Know that I have transferred the seat of the bishopric of Dorchester to the City of Lincoln by the authority and advice of Pope Alexander and also of his legates and of Archbishop Lanfranc and of the other bishops of my kingdom, and that I have given sufficient land there, free and quit of all customary dues for the construction of a mother church of the whole diocese and its ancillary buildings . . . . .'

Silver pennies minted in Lincoln (actual size)

Edward the Confessor; moneyer Auti

Edward the Confessor; moneyer Gifel

William I; moneyer Gifel

William also favoured an Englishman named Colsuen. We do not know why, but we do know that after 1068 Colsuen became one of the most important people in the kingdom and one of the only two Englishmen to have the rank of baron. William gave him generous gifts of land, much of it around Lincoln.

On the other hand, some important Englishmen had their Lincoln property taken from them. For example, Ernuin the priest, who may have been one of King Edward the Confessor's chaplains, had his twenty-two houses, two churches and land in Stamford taken from him, though he was given land in the village of Ingham as well as a house in Lincoln.

Then there were the lawmen who had studied law, and could explain it when asked. Many laws had never been written down; few people could read the laws that *were* written, so the lawmen would have been asked for advice by people who were willing to pay for it. In this way they became wealthy and powerful in the city. We do not know why, but William confiscated all the property of two of the lawmen and gave it to two of his own followers from Normandy: Peter of Valognes and Crassus. He allowed the others to carry on undisturbed.

Moneyers, too, had to be trustworthy as they were licensed to coin. They melted silver and alloy together and cut out flans and hammered them into dies. These coins, called pennies, had the king's portrait stamped on one side, and on the other the mint name of Lincoln and the name of the moneyer who had made them. William allowed all seven moneyers to keep their positions and even appointed six other Englishmen to join them.

7

The castle

As well as the cathedral, William ordered the building of Lincoln castle. One hundred and sixty-six houses close to the western wall of the city were destroyed to make room for an earthern mound topped first by a wooden stockade then by a stone tower. This mound, and a space at its foot (about 2.4 hectares, or 6 acres), was surrounded on three sides by earth banks 6 to 9 metres (20-30 ft) high, outside of which was a dry ditch 50 to 70 metres (55–75 yards) broad. The cliff dropped so steeply on the south-west side that there was no need for either bank or ditch.

In this enclosed space, called the inner bail, the garrison on duty lived in tents or in wooden huts. Their horses would have been kept in a stockade in the inner bail, and their food, drink and weapons would also probably have been stored there.

It is possible that Colsuen was the first constable of Lincoln castle. The constable acted for the king in the military defence of the city. Everyone had to treat him as if he were the king. His duty was to see that the castle was garrisoned, and in time of danger he had to take command and hold it for the king. To do this, he had to have knights to help him. To get this help he paid some knights eight pence a day. He gave other knights land but no money. This land was called a *knight's fee* and the knights and their families were expected to live off the produce from the fee. The bishop of Lincoln also owed knight service to the king.

Sometimes a man who held land from the bishop or constable paid money to be excused castle guard service, so that he was allowed to stay at home. One such was John de Rye, who held a fee from the bishop and owed five shillings and five pence for not doing guard service at Lincoln castle.

No knights were supposed to be asked to do more than forty days' service in the year, or to serve overseas.

The Lincoln garrison did more than stay inside the castle. In 1069 a Danish invasion was joined by Edgar the Aetheling (see page 5) and some of his followers, and together they sailed up the Humber and entered York. The Aetheling went on a separate plundering expedition into Lindsey and his party was unexpectedly attacked by the Lincoln garrison, who took most of them prisoner and destroyed their ship. Only the Aetheling and two companions escaped this surprise attack.

Before the battle of 1066 William ordered a castle to be built at Hastings. The Bayeux tapestry shows men piling up the earth mound. On top is a stockade.

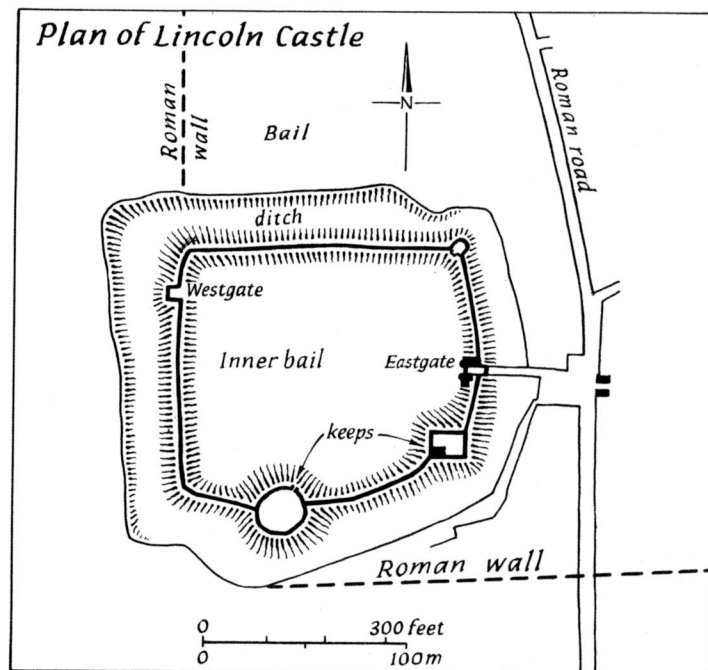

Plan of Lincoln Castle

8

A bird's eye view of Lincoln castle as it may have been in Norman times. You can see the second, or shell, keep which was added soon after the first. The mound or 'motte' of the shell keep is about 6 m (20 ft) high and 30.5 m (100 ft) across.

below: A nineteenth-century engraving of the west gate of the castle built in the reign of Henry I near the site of the old Roman west gate.

Earth mounds were built up over the ruins of some of the Roman walls. At first there may have been wooden fences on top of the mounds; soon new stone walls were built. Here is part of the Norman wall, laid in 'herring-bone' pattern.

The houses in the town

All towns were said to belong to the king. Houses built within a town or city were regarded as particularly valuable, because the king allowed walls and castles to be built for their protection.

Most of these houses were wooden with straw thatched roofs. You can see some in the drawing on page 4. A few had glass in the windows; most only had wooden shutters to keep out the wind and the rain. They were heated by log fires, which burned all the year round on the hearthstone in the middle of the room. There were no chimneys. The smoke from the fires seeped out through a hole in the roof. As the risk of fire was great, William ordered a 'curfew' (*couvre feu* or 'cover fire'). At sunset the biggest bell in each church was tolled as a signal for every fire to be covered over with its own ashes. After this people were not allowed to go out of doors unless they had permission to do so, or were on the king's business.

The homes, rich and poor alike, had little furniture and few utensils. The wooden furniture consisted chiefly of chests, tables, stools and benches. Rich and important people would have a bed, chests and a few chairs. Chests were the commonest furniture. Clothes, books, charters, money and jewellery were all stored in chests and the lids served as beds, benches and tables. The earliest chests were true 'trunks' made from sections of hollowed-out tree trunks, but by 1068 'cofferers' were making rough boxes of hand-cut planks joined together with wooden pegs.

Chairs were simply chests with the backs and sides extended. They were rare and were used only by important people, so they became a sign of authority. This is the origin of the word 'chairman'.

Tables were simply broad boards laid on trestles and could be cleared away after meals.

Nearly everyone would have kept a few hens, a goose or two, or a goat, or pig, on the plot of land on which the house stood. On the plot, or even on the house roof, grew pot herbs: sage, marjoram, bay, houseleeks and soapwort, or fullers' grass. Fullers' grass was a remedy for cuts and bruises, and was also handy for personal cleanliness before the invention of soap. Bees kept in beeskeps (straw hives) gave honey for sweetening food and for use as a preservative.

We know there were 1,150 houses in Lincoln in 1069 and by 1086 there were more than 5,000 people. Many houses belonged to freemen or burgesses of the city. The freemen were the next important class of people in Lincoln, and one degree below knights.

above: *Preparing the evening meal. A poor family's home probably looked similar to this inside. A modern artist's impression.*

left: *A chest which has been axed or burnt out of the solid trunk of an oak tree. The chest is now in Howden church in Yorkshire. It was probably made soon after 1300, but was made in the old style which was normal in the eleventh century.*

In this picture which is taken from the April page of an eleventh-century calendar we see three very important men. We know they are important because they are sitting on a cushioned seat which has a high wooden back and arms carved into animal shapes. Each man holds a differently shaped drinking mug. All three are wearing cloaks around their shoulders, and soft shoes that fit closely around their ankles. They are resting their feet on a long wooden foot rest. As this has arched outlets at regular intervals, it is possible that shallow pans of charcoal were burning underneath it to warm their feet. The other people in the picture are probably servants in attendance to pour out drinks and entertain with music.

below: The drawings of sage, bay and marjoram are from Gerard's Herbal 1597. The crop plants on the next page are from the same book. The beeskeps are from an an edition of Vergil's 'Georgics' published in Strasburg in 1502. These are about the earliest pictures that try to show plants with any real accuracy. In the eleventh century everybody was probably as familiar with herbs as we are with ordinary vegetables.

Houseleeks

Sage

Baytree

Marjoram

Beeskeps

Wheat   Rye

Two more pictures from the calendar shown on page 11. The one above is for the month of January and shows a wooden plough pulled by four oxen.

Oxen were strong animals but slow moving and docile enough to be guided and controlled by a young boy using a long stick-like whip. The oxen are harnessed in pairs on either side of a long centre pole stretching out from the plough's axle. The plough wheels were made entirely of wood. The ploughshare too was wooden and so was the mould board. This made it very heavy and meant that it took all one person's strength to hold it steady on course and through the soil.

Freemen and taxes

A man became a freeman if his father was free, or by living for a year and a day in Lincoln, and by paying a land tax called *land-gable* of a penny a year, to the bailiff. The bailiff was a freeman appointed to be the king's representative in the city. One man who, we know, became a freeman and bailiff was Ralph the Villein who was bailiff of Lincoln for four years. Probably freemen did not do castle guard, although those living in the Bail, near the castle, had to pay something towards the hire of the knights.

Freemen did, however, have to repair the city walls, or they had to pay another tax called *murage* which was used to hire skilled stonemasons to do the work.

Payment of land-gable usually meant that each freeman held a plot of land within the city boundary, clearly defined in area and called a *burgage tenement*. He could leave this land to his children or other relatives, he could mortgage it, or he could sell it or give it to someone else. In addition, a freeman held and farmed four to six strips in the open land outside the city walls. The strips were usually a furlong long and four rods wide (an acre, or about 200 m by 20 m). Wheat, barley, rye, oats, vetches, peas and beans were the commonest crops. Freemen were also allowed, by 'the Stint' (the restriction on the number of animals to be grazed), to graze three beasts on the common pasture, which was not very extensive, while other people were allowed to graze only one.

This restriction on the amount of livestock was necessary as Lincoln had only 100 acres, or 40 hectares of meadow on which to grow hay. This hay, with the chaff from the bread grains, and the bines (stems) from the peas and beans, was the

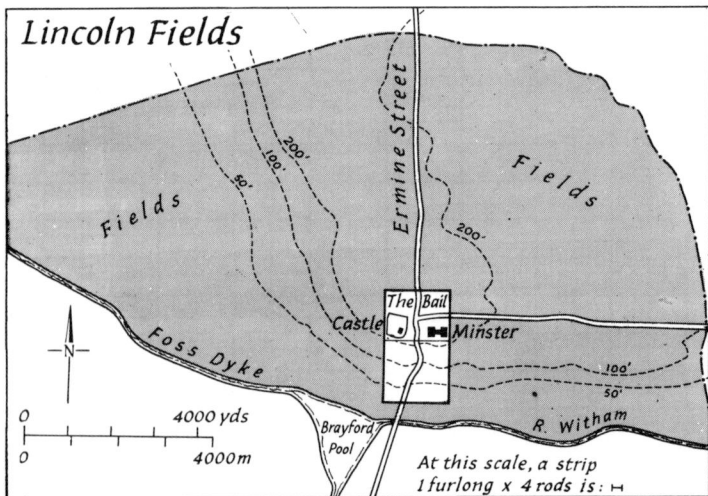

Lincoln Fields

At this scale, a strip
1 furlong x 4 rods is:

Peas

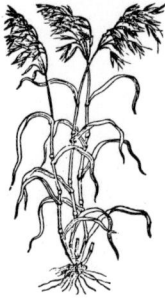

Oats

only winter feed for the animals of the city, or for visitors' horses and for the livestock driven to market.

All the freemen were required to attend every meeting of the borough court or *burwarmot* (borough-moot, or borough-meeting). As nearly all buildings were small this assembly was held out of doors, probably in the churchyard of St Peter ad Placita, which stood just to the east of the main street, Mikelgate. The burwarmot met regularly to deal with the day-to-day management of the city and was presided over by the king's bailiff. A clerk who could read, write and 'reckon' had to be present at all meetings because it was necessary to keep a record. Also the advice of the lawmen about points of law would be recorded as a guide for future decisions.

The burwarmot must have spent some time discussing and settling each freeman's share of the money that the city owed the king. Before the Norman Conquest, Lincoln owed the king £20 a year. However, prices had risen and William had need of money to keep his army in fighting trim so he increased this amount to £100 which had to be paid even in years when the harvests were poor and business bad.

The land-gable was reckoned as part of this sum of £100, but one penny from each of the 1,150 freemen then added up to only £4 15s 10d. This meant that the freemen had to find the difference out of their own purses and the king's bailiff was there to see that they did so.

Money was scarce. Poor people who were lucky enough to get work probably worked six days a week and earned only a penny a day. Whether they helped to build the castle or cathedral, drove sheep and cattle to market, carted food into

This picture is for August and shows men harvesting corn. Three of them have sickles to cut the grain stalks. Two of these men hold the sickle in their left hands, the third in his right. A fourth man is picking the corn off the ground. A fifth is carrying a sheaf to the cart. The others are loading the cart. The wheels are made with eight spokes and eight felloes each.

the city or served as foot soldiers at the castle they all earned the same. Yet people saved money, and set themselves up in trade or entered professions such as that of priest.

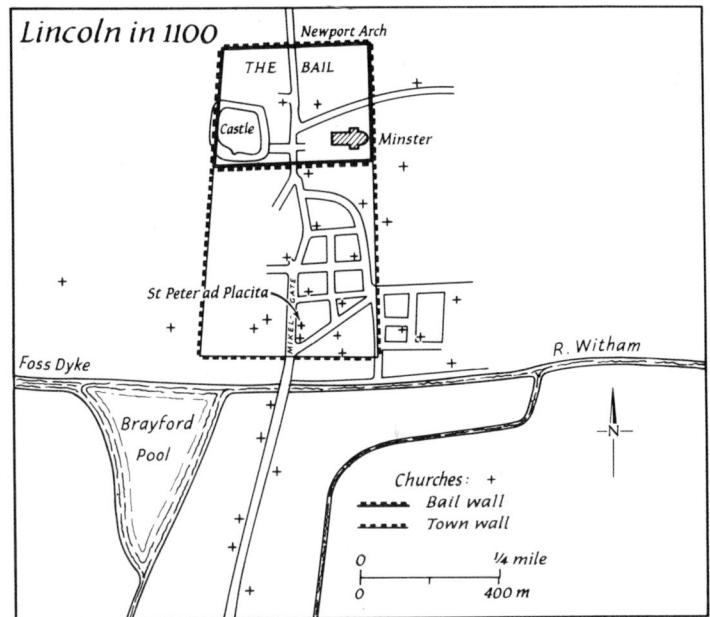

Lincoln in 1100

The Church

Only five churches are recorded as established in Lincoln in 1068, possibly because they were the only ones built of stone. There were other ones, probably built of wood. Stone or wood, these churches had few windows and therefore were dark inside. They were thatched, like the houses, or roofed with wooden shingles, and inside and out were decorated with paintings and carvings. The church bells were usually hung in stone towers. As the map on page 13 shows, there were many more parish churches by 1100.

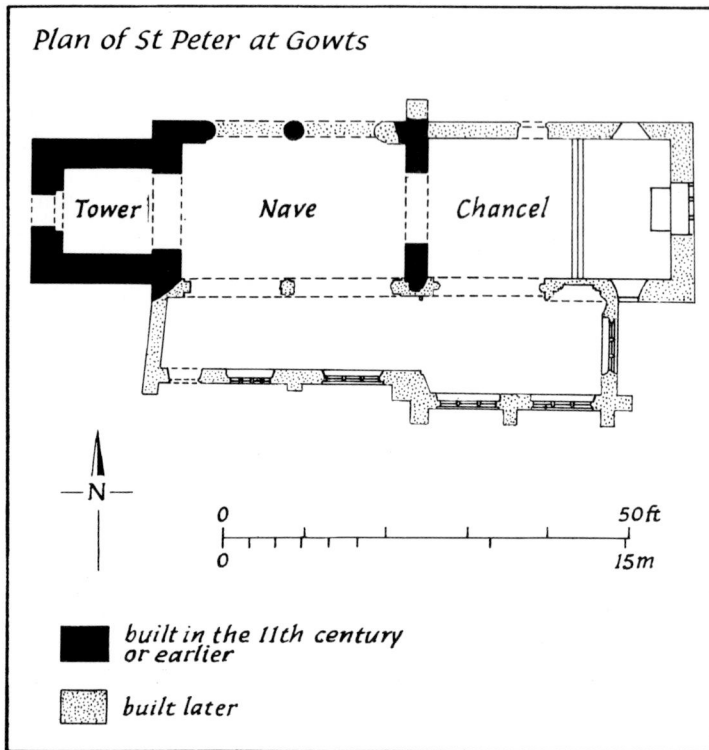

Plan of St Peter at Gowts

Tower | Nave | Chancel

—N—

0   50 ft

0   15 m

■ built in the 11th century or earlier

▨ built later

The tower of the church of St Peter at Gowts (gowts means gutters) was probably built about AD 950. It is about 22 m high and is built of small stones laid closely together with dressed stone blocks for corners and windows.

An artist's idea of what the west front of Remigius's new cathedral would have looked like. It was finished by 1092. Standing on the top of the ridge to the east of the castle, the cathedral with its great towers and 99 metre-long nave is a landmark to the whole countryside.

As you can see from the other pictures in this book, elaborate carvings and pointed arches were later added to the west front but some of the arches of Remigius's facade can still be seen.

Leisure time

The parish churches were not only places of worship, they were also social centres for the people who lived round about. But because they and the houses were small and dark inside, the people of Lincoln spent as much time as possible out of doors. Even shopping, for example, was mostly done out of doors. The shops were often nothing more than open-fronted booths on the ground floor of the houses in which the shopkeepers lived.

The streets were where the people played various games. A kind of football played with a leather ball stuffed with rags or straw was popular. Archery contests, horse races and other tests of skill were held. Hunting or hawking around the city became the favourite outdoor sport of the knights.

By the beginning of the thirteenth century, Lincoln had become a major regional centre. The town was the focus of a growing road system and many inns were built to offer accommodation to travellers. Pilgrims, church officials, legal officers, tax collectors and merchants were all regular visitors to Lincoln's inns bringing business and money to the town.

Performing bears were a popular form of street entertainment. A women dances in front of the bear, trying to avoid the bear seizing her. The unmuzzled bear is further irritated by the jester standing behind. An engraving based on a fourteenth-century manuscript.

In the time of Magna Carta

King John rides into Lincoln, 1216

2 In the time of Magna Carta

In the century after the Norman Conquest many changes took place in English towns. A few, such as Thetford (see map on page 5), declined in importance and population. Most existing towns grew in size, while many new ones appeared or were granted royal charters and the right to hold markets.

The chief change that had taken place in the population of Lincoln by 1216, when King John paid his last visit, was the increased number of *foreigners* who lived there. Foreigners were those men and women who had not been born in Lincoln but who had come either from neighbouring villages, or from other countries. Such were William de Fiskerton, Gilbert of Lissington, Nicholas of Chester, Walter le Fleming and William de Paris. In particular, there were the Jews.

The Jews

By 1216, the Jews formed a small but important part of Lincoln's population. They did not mix with the other inhabitants. They were not allowed to be freemen, belong to guilds or have any trade except that of goldsmith. They were called 'the King's Persons' and officially they and their property belonged to the king. Many Jews became rich because they were money-lenders, which Church law forbade Christians to be. However, by the end of the thirteenth century, growing hostility from people who owed money to the Jews made royal protection of them unwise and in 1290 Edward I expelled the Jews from England.

One of the most famous of the Lincoln Jews was Aaron, who died a few years before King John came to the throne. He had been very rich, and when he died many people and several institutions, including the bishop of Lincoln and nine Cistercian abbeys, owed him money. Because he was a 'King's Person', the king was his heir. A special branch of the royal Exchequer was set up to collect Aaron's money.

Another well-known Jew in Lincoln was Belaset, the daughter of Solomon of Wallingford, who was accused of 'clipping the king's coin' – trimming the rough edges of coins with a knife and melting down the trimmings. She was tried in London and sentenced to death, although some thought that the evidence had been trumped up because she was a money-lender. She was hanged outside the Jews' Court in Lincoln, as an example to other Jews.

Guilds

With this influx of 'foreigners' who brought new trades and skills the freemen realised that they would be better off if they banded together in some sort of special Lincoln organisation. They had formed the Guild Merchant during the reign of John's father, Henry II, who had granted them a charter. As a result, any merchant who was not an inhabitant of the city had to trade through the Guild Merchant. In order to prevent competition among the guild members, they agreed to regard each other as brothers, and soon they came to be called 'the Brethren'.

It was possible for people who had remained in the city for a year and a day, with their right to live there unchallenged, to become free and subsequently to buy their way into a trade. Hence many different trades grew up in Lincoln. These trades were governed by rules made by the guilds. There were all kinds of guilds: religious guilds, social guilds and craft guilds as well as the Guild Merchant. They were all different yet they all tried in their own ways to keep up a high standard of workmanship by a rigid inspection system in each separate guild. Each guild gave its members protection, an annual dinner, help with money when they were sick and a fine funeral. It also decided how people could qualify for membership.

In craft guilds there were three grades of membership: apprentices, journeymen and masters. Wax candles, which were expensive, were always valuable to guild members, so

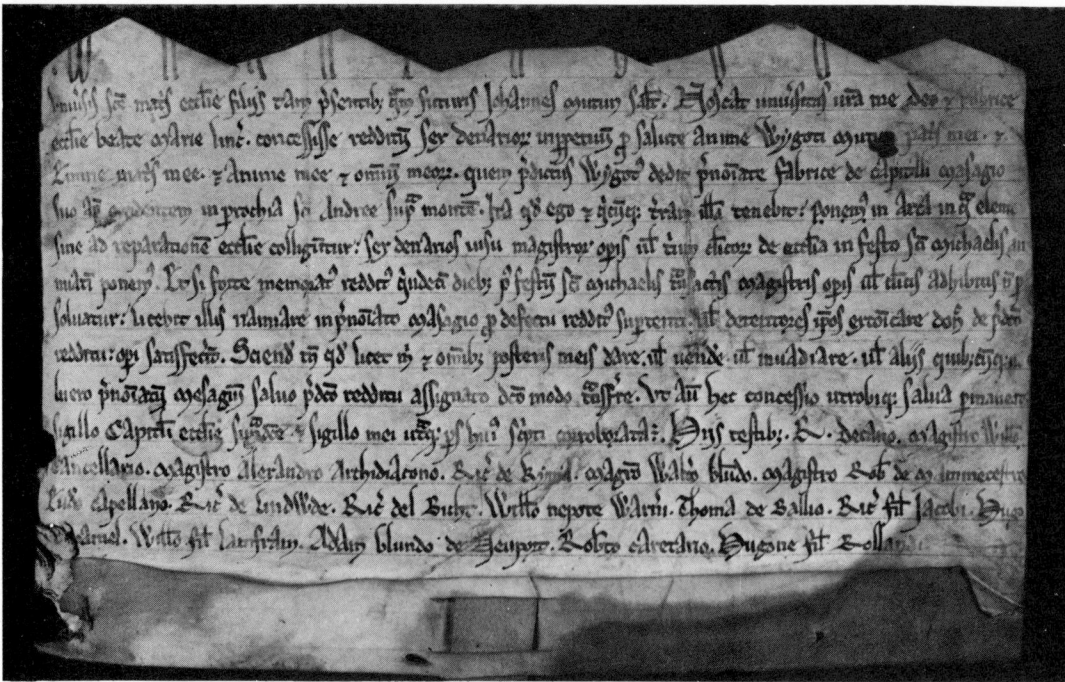

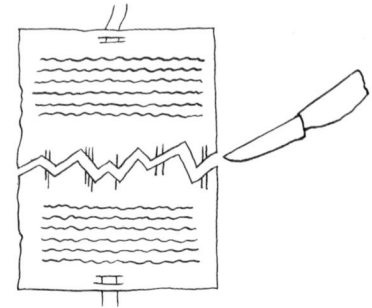

An indenture was a contract written out twice on one piece of parchment. This was then cut into two pieces, great care being taken to make sure that the cut left a jagged, 'indented', edge. This was to prevent forgery. If there was a dispute about a contract the two pieces of parchment could be fitted together to prove that they belonged together.

No apprenticeship indenture survives from medieval Lincoln but there is one drawn up about 1217 by John Muntun and the dean and chapter of the cathedral. John Muntun agrees to pay towards the upkeep of the cathedral an annual rent of 6d from his property in the parish of St Andrew on the Hill.

anyone who wished to learn a craft had to pay a penny 'to the wax', as it was called, before a brother could teach him. Having paid his penny he became an apprentice, and his teacher was his master. 'Indentures', or contracts, were drawn up between them.

In the contract the master agreed to teach the apprentice the craft, to provide him with clothing, and with board and lodging. In return the apprentice had to obey his master and work for him as long as the apprenticeship lasted, usually a period of seven years.

When his time was up the apprentice became a journeyman which meant that he could be employed at a daily wage fixed by his guild, generally three pence. The word 'journeyman' comes from the French word *journée* (day). Now he could marry if he wished. In order to become a master a journeyman had to make a 'masterpiece' and submit it for examination by all the masters of his craft guild. Relatively few did this because of the expense of buying the necessary materials. Also, if admitted to a guild as 'master' he had to pay an entrance fee and provide a 'feast' for all the members of the guild.

There were three craft guilds in Lincoln by 1216: the Weavers' Guild, the Fullers' Guild, and the Dyers' Guild. Together, these three craft guilds made and dyed blankets and cloth. You probably know what weavers and dyers did but the fullers' share is not so obvious. They washed the woven cloth and then pegged it out on the ground so that they could brush up the nap to make the cloth fluffy. They did this with a kind of

A mason and a carpenter are making their test pieces (or masterpieces) before the warden of a guild in the hope that they will be admitted as masters. From a fifteenth-century Flemish manuscript. Though the costumes would vary somewhat, the same scene must often have been repeated all over Europe throughout the Middle Ages.

below: *The hall of the great religious and social guild of St Mary. It was built about 1180. The wide gateway gave on to a courtyard at the back. In this hall the guild held business meetings, official courts and feasts and stored their goods and records.*

thistle called a teazel. The most expensive cloth was the 'Lincoln scarlet'. It was dyed by crushing a small insect called a 'greyne' and mixing it with water. In 1181 the sheriff of Lincoln bought ninety ells (about 100 metres) of this cloth for £30.

The mayor

The city's day-to-day management was still carried out by the freemen, meeting together in the burwarmot, which, in 1216, was presided over by a new civic official – the mayor – and two bailiffs. The burwarmot met once a week. There is no record of any of its members being paid for their services, but the city now had to pay £180 a year to the king.

The mayor, like the bishop and the constable of the castle, was one of the most important people in Lincoln. He was responsible to the king for the good behaviour of the people and for their protection against injustice.

The changes came about like this. In 1194 the freemen of Lincoln bought a charter from King Richard I for 500 marks (a mark was worth 13s 4d) which allowed them to hold the burwarmot once a week and to choose their own bailiff to work with the bailiff appointed by the king.

Five years later the Lincoln freemen bought a charter from King John. It cost 300 marks. This charter directed that the citizens might choose both bailiffs. It also set up ten new civic officials.

Four of 'the more lawful and discreet citizens' were to be chosen as coroners. Their first duty was to see that all the court cases which the king claimed should be tried only in the presence of his appointed judges, were so heard. They also had to see that the bailiffs treated rich and poor justly and lawfully.

Four *bedells* (beadles) of the city were to attend upon the mayor and the court of the burwarmot, to keep the peace and to execute legal processes. There were to be two clerks of the city, to draw up deeds, to keep the court records and to conduct official correspondence. It was to win these privileges that the citizens had to increase their annual payment from £100 to £180.

From all this we can see that by 1216 Lincoln was a corporation. That is, the citizens had become united into a body which had all the rights of a single individual. As few people could read but all could recognise symbols it is probable the city now had an official seal for letters and documents.

Furthermore, the citizens must have agreed at a meeting of the burwarmot to pay money into a 'common' purse so that they could all benefit. For instance they could use the money to buy themselves more privileges. Finally, the citizens delegated their authority to a mayor and 'Common' Council.

The city records show that from 1206 the mayor had had an advisory council called the Common Council. We do not know how this council was recruited. Perhaps the mayor and

A drawing of Lincoln's mayoral seal. It shows the Virgin Mary crowned and standing beneath an arch. On either side are the leopards of England. The inscription reads: 'Sigill Maioritatis Lincolnie' (seal of the mayoralty of Lincoln). The seal dates from about 1300.

Right: *One of the four surviving copies of Magna Carta. The barons who drew up Magna Carta as a guarantee of the privileges and liberties of all free Englishmen sent copies to all the main towns. This copy is 38 centimetres square, and is still preserved in Lincoln.*

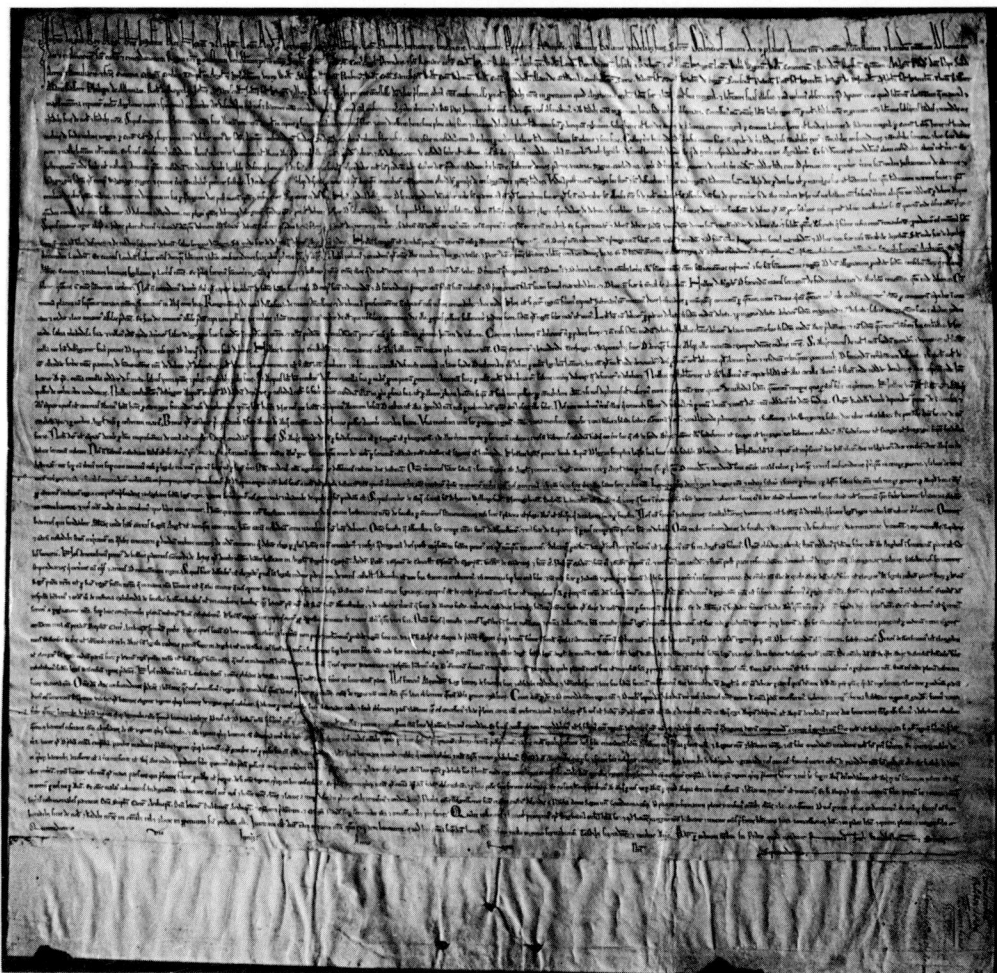

bailiffs found people from among their friends and relations who were willing to serve. The records show that some members held office for a long time, others served for a few years and then dropped out, and a few served only once.

The king still could veto all or any of the city's appointments, and he still had his royal officer, the sheriff, to supervise the administration of justice in Lincoln. The sheriff was not the same as the constable of the castle though the two jobs could be held by the same person, and were, at this time, by a remarkable lady named Nicholaa de la Haye. As sheriff she had to see that punishments were legal and that fines were duly paid.

We know that Lincoln had a mayor in 1206 but we are given no name until 1210 when the citizens paid £100 to the royal Exchequer that they might have Adam as mayor, as long as he should please the king and serve him well. Adam had obviously displeased the king in 1212 for he was fined 500 marks and the whole of Lincoln was taxed to pay this money while the bailiffs, Thomas of Paris and Ralph, stood surety. There is some evidence that Adam supported the barons in their quarrel against the king.

Lincoln was very much involved in the quarrel which had begun in 1207 when Pope Innocent III chose Stephen Langton as archbishop of Canterbury. King John would not accept Stephen Langton, so in 1208 the pope placed England under an interdict. When, in the following year, John chose Hugh of Wells to be the new bishop of Lincoln, he told Hugh to seek consecration from the archbishop of Rouen in France. Instead, Hugh was consecrated by John's enemy, Stephen Langton, so the king dismissed Hugh from office.

Later, the king made peace with the pope, but then his barons rebelled against him and in 1214 a baronial army assembled in Lincoln. Meanwhile the main baronial army, which was accompanied by Stephen Langton and Hugh of Wells, captured London. Finally his enemies all met King John and on 15 June 1215 he was forced to accept Magna Carta at Runnymede, on the River Thames. One of the four surviving copies may be seen still in Lincoln cathedral library.

John now appealed to the pope, who issued a bull of excommunication against 'the disturbers of the country'. Adam of Lincoln was expressly named as one of these. Adam was dismissed from office as mayor in 1216, just after John's last visit to the city.

The houses in the town

Adam of Lincoln is known to have had houses in the suburb of Wigford as well as in Hungate and in the Bail. The city itself was walled, but now suburbs had grown up outside the walls. Either the people who lived in them wanted more land than was available inside the city walls or they hoped to escape from the sounds and smells of the market.

Look back at the map of Lincoln in 1100 on page 13. What areas of the city have grown in importance during the past century?

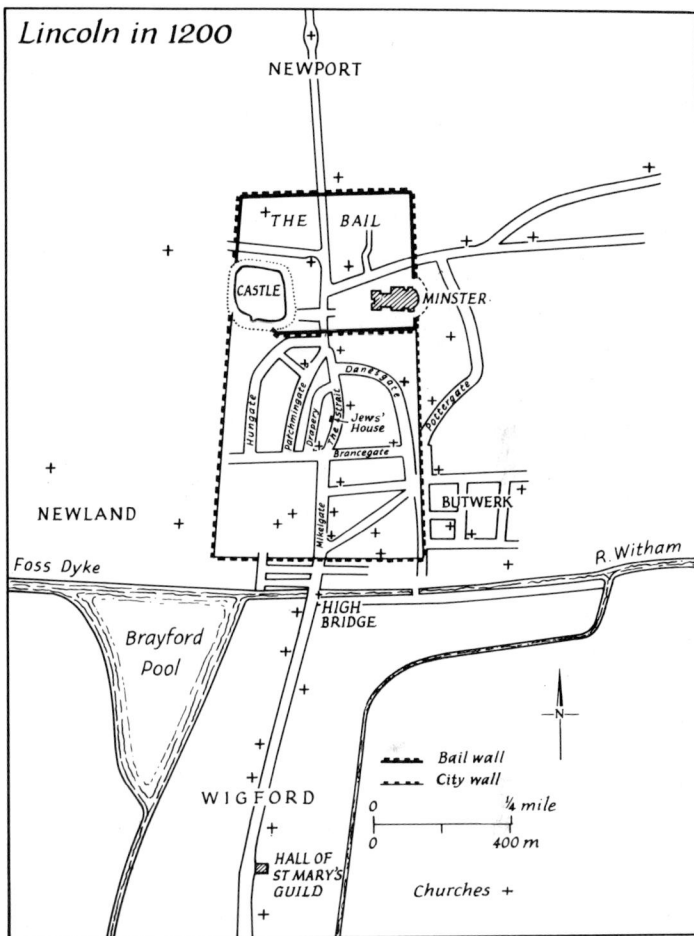

Lincoln in 1200

In 1122 a fire had destroyed a great part of Lincoln, so there had been much rebuilding. We can learn about these new buildings by examining a house of this period, now known as 'the Jews' House'. It is two-storeyed with a steeply pitched roof. The main door is on the ground floor and the family would have entered along a narrow passage between the ground floor store-rooms to an annexe at the back where there were stairs up to the main living room on the first floor. This room had a fireplace built into the wall immediately over the front door. There was no chimney though; the smoke escaped through flues coming out on each side of the outside buttress. The kitchen was on the ground floor. The stores would have included fodder for the animals owned by the family. The furniture and utensils were still very simple. In the wealthier houses carpets were hung on the walls to keep out the draught.

One of the reasons why the Jews built such strong stone houses (the walls of this one are a metre thick) was to protect their valuables against thieves and fire. Another reason would be to protect themselves against a frequently hostile town population.

The Jews' house, No. 15 The Strait, Lincoln, built about 1180. The chimneys were added later.

A fireplace with the flue in the buttress behind it.

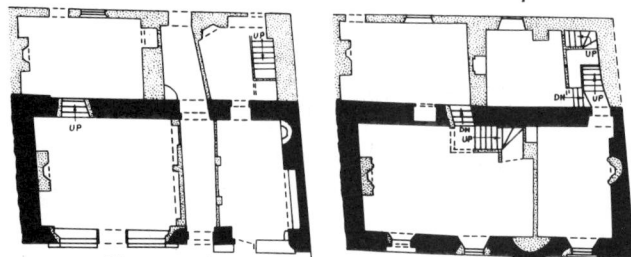

Plan of the Jews' House

Ground plan   floor plan

The Strait

0   10   20   30 feet
0   5   10m

■ 12th century   ▨ built later

above: *A detail of the carving over the doorway at the Jews' House.*

above right: *Thirteenth-century pottery made in Lincoln. The tallest jug is 35 cm high.*

Servants are drawing water from a well and carrying it upstairs. You can see the weighted counter-balance which helped to raise the bucket. On the left is an elaborately decorated cupboard. Redrawn from a twelfth-century manuscript.

23

The castle

Building had also altered both the castle walls and yard. Stone walls had been raised on top of the earth banks. These had now been completed on the south-west, making the inner bailey a totally enclosed place. The motte, topped by a shell keep had also been added in the south-west angle of the wall. The shell keep was a stone wall encircling a small space which could be defended independently of the other parts of the castle. Look again at the drawing on page 9.

All this may have helped Nicholaa de la Haye, Colsuen's great-granddaughter, to remain loyal to King John and to hold the castle for him. Nicholaa de la Haye became constable of the castle and sheriff of the city in 1216. Her husband Gerard de Camville had died in 1215 and their only son in 1216. When King John arrived in Lincoln, Nicholaa came out of the castle and offered the keys to the king, saying that she was a woman of great age and could no longer bear the burden of office. The king handed them back to her to hold 'until I shall order otherwise'. This is the first known official recognition given to a woman in a high position in local government.

Before King John died, Prince Louis of France, who had allied himself with the English barons who were fighting against King John, made an attempt to seize the English

throne. A party of his troops took the city of Lincoln, though the castle, commanded by Nicholaa de la Haye, fought them off. Louis failed to make Nicholaa yield the castle and soon returned to London, and then to France. Nicholaa de la Haye finally resigned the constableship of the castle in 1226. She died four years later.

left: *Steps lead from the inner bailey to the entrance of the shell keep. Instead of the square tower erected on the earlier motte this keep wall has fifteen sides and so avoids the sharp angles that were easy to attack and hard to defend. The walls had a rampart walk with a parapet around the top. The space inside was open to the sky but there were probably timber buildings against the walls.*

below: *The east gate of the castle was probably strengthened after the fighting in 1217. The two turrets were originally higher and a barbican, or outer defence, was built in front of the gate. Only fragments of this remain in the modern wall on the left of the road.*

There is now no trace of any building in which Nicholaa de la Haye might have lived, within the castle walls. Nor is there anything left of a house she inherited in the suburb, Newport.

Around Newport husbandmen, or smallholders, farmed the city's lands, paying rent to the knights or freemen and selling the produce of the land.

From the castle, King John probably moved across the Bail to the cathedral. Here he would have been greeted by the bishop with the dean and the canons, the teachers and pupils of the theological school, the grammar school and the song school. He would have been shown the progress of the great work of re-building which had been begun by a famous Lincoln 'foreigner', Bishop (later St) Hugh.

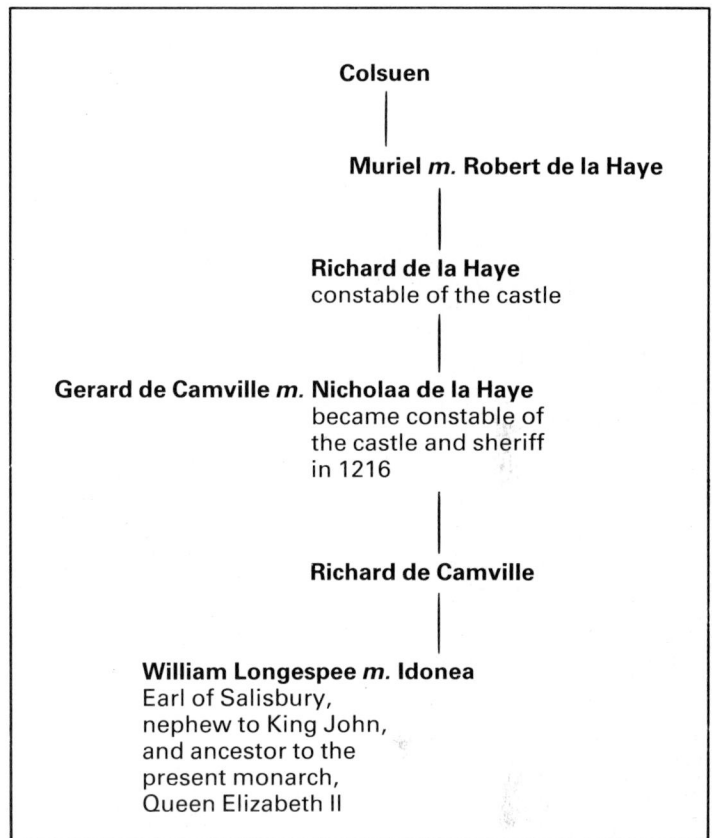

Colsuen
|
Muriel *m.* Robert de la Haye
|
Richard de la Haye
constable of the castle
|
Gerard de Camville *m.* Nicholaa de la Haye
became constable of
the castle and sheriff
in 1216
|
Richard de Camville
|
William Longespee *m.* Idonea
Earl of Salisbury,
nephew to King John,
and ancestor to the
present monarch,
Queen Elizabeth II

This table shows how Nicholaa de la Haye was descended from Colsuen.

The statue of St Hugh on the south pinnacle of the west front of the cathedral. The present statue dates from the eighteenth century when the pinnacles were restored after a storm.

Hugh, Bishop of Lincoln

Hugh was born in Avalon in France. When he grew up he became a monk and was soon appointed prior of an English monastery. Here he became so successful that King Henry II offered him the bishopric of Lincoln. The king had to make the offer three times before Hugh accepted. He became bishop in 1186.

When he became bishop, Hugh found the cathedral in ruins as a result of a fire in 1141 and an earthquake in 1185. He had no money with which to rebuild it. Probably because of this he issued a mandate to the archdeacons of his diocese to encourage people to bring offerings to the 'Mother' church of Lincoln. The names of some of these people who made donations are written in the great Bible. King John's name does not appear, although we know he gave trees from Sherwood Forest.

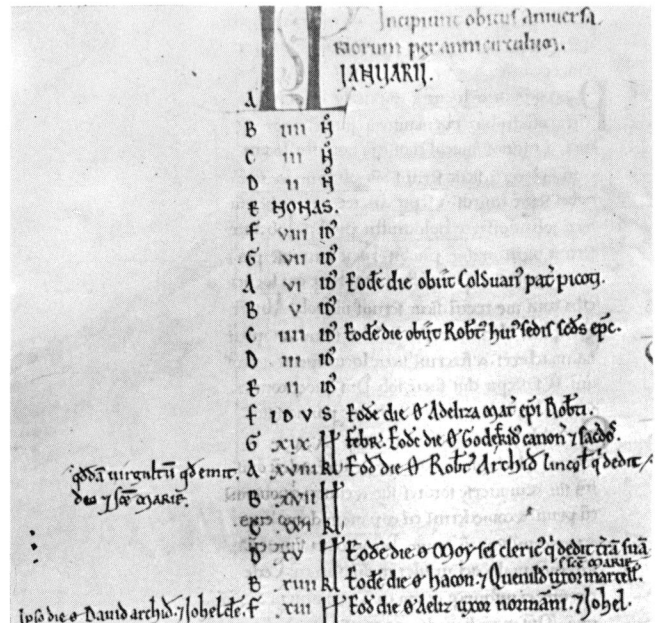

In the cathedral's twelfth-century Bible there is a calendar which records the deaths of the bishops, canons and those who gave money to the building of the cathedral. This is part of the list for January. Note Colsuen's name and the Roman system of dates.

Plan of Lincoln Cathedral

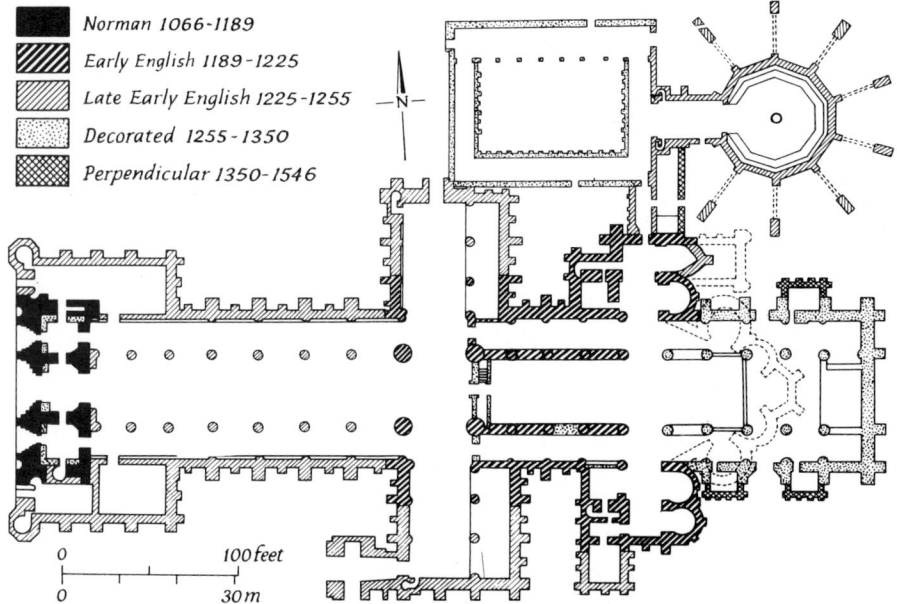

- ■ Norman 1066-1189
- ▨ Early English 1189-1225
- ▨ Late Early English 1225-1255
- ▥ Decorated 1255-1350
- ▨ Perpendicular 1350-1546

0   100 feet
0   30 m

The swineherd of Stow. An old story tells how the swineherd gave his life savings of sixteen silver pennies towards the building of the cathedral. In return, St Hugh promised that his effigy would stand forever in the cathedral as a memorial to his generosity. This picture shows the original statue of the swineherd, which now stands in the cloister. In 1851 Joshua Byron was paid 5s a day, for 7½ days, to carve a 'colossal' figure to replace the original statue, which was badly eroded by the weather. The new statue stands on a pinnacle on the west front, opposite that of St Hugh.

right: *The nave of the cathedral looking from the choir down to the west door.*

The building work was directed by the Frenchman Geoffrey of Noiers but Bishop Hugh organised the whole operation, contributed to the building fund himself and even, it said, carried stones for the masons. The work was begun in 1192 almost exactly 100 years after the completion of Bishop Remigius's cathedral.

Hugh died in 1200 (16 years before King John's last visit to Lincoln) and he was proclaimed a saint by the Church in 1220. As the cathedral was still incomplete neither Hugh nor King John saw it in all its glory.

In the time of the Hundred Years War

Edward III rides into Lincoln, 1327. What principal changes can you see between Lincoln in 1216 (page 16) and 1327?

3 From King John to the Black Death

After Magna Carta, many new towns came into existence. Edward I founded several new towns and boroughs. Old towns grew, suburbs developed and it became necessary for pass-laws to limit the numbers of visitors and pilgrims to some towns. Lincoln had stone walls and gates built. These are shown on the map on page 30. By the end of the thirteenth century, trade and industry had begun to decline in England. Many towns stopped growing and some new towns were never lived in. But for Lincoln, this continued to be a time of great prosperity, as this chapter shows. The town's wealth increased, as did its importance as a market centre. Lincoln's growth came to an end with the outbreak of the Black Death in 1349.

Edward III comes to Lincoln

Foreigners, by trading in Lincoln, had made it so important a city by the fourteenth century that Edward III held his first parliament in the cathedral chapter house in 1327. Lincoln was represented in each medieval parliament by two men. In 1301 these were William Cause and Stephen Stanham. William Cause was also mayor. In 1327 the Lincoln men summoned to parliament were John de Tame and William de Hackthorn.

These non-baronial members of parliament could not vote. They could only petition the king in matters concerning their city, listen to what discussion there was, inform their fellow citizens at a meeting of the burwarmot what taxes they had to pay, and see that the king's commands were carried out.

The civic party that would have greeted King Edward III would have been much larger than that which had greeted King John. There would have been: the members of parliament; the mayor of the 'Staple', William de Spaigne; the ponderator; four chamberlains; two constables from each parish; as well as the mayor, Common Council and the other civic officials. (You can read about the new officials on pages 35 and 36.)

The dean and chapter and the representatives of other religious bodies in Lincoln would have accompanied the bishop when he greeted the king at the Exchequer gate, the main entrance into 'the Close', because, by 1327, the Close had its own walls.

Edward III was the first English king to issue gold coinage. This coin, called a rose noble, was worth 6s 8d, or 80 silver pennies. Parliament called Edward III the 'King of the Sea'. In 1338 he claimed the throne of France, hence the shield shows the lilies of France with the leopards of England (2½ times actual size).

The Bail was already walled. The constable of the castle, Ebulo Lestrange, would have waited for the king by the eastern gateway of the castle.

From 1216 the constable of the castle had held a separate court, a court baron, for his tenants in the Bail, and had rented parts of the castle ditches to merchants and had allowed the setting up of market stalls there. These rents were valuable as income so the city's mayors and bailiffs wanted to add this money to the Lincoln 'Common' purse and therefore tried to assert their authority in the Bail. In 1322 the bailiffs of Lincoln complained to the king that they were prevented from doing their duty in the Bail by the order of the constable of the castle. Nine years later King Edward III commanded them to allow Alice de Lacy (a descendant of Nicholaa de la Haye) and her husband, Ebulo Lestrange, custody and ward of the castle with the Bail, to have their court baron there, the assay of weights and measures for the city, and all other profits. So the bailiffs lost.

The Bail had encircled the cathedral built by Remigius but when Bishop Hugh rebuilt the cathedral he extended it eastwards. This had meant that he had part of the city wall, which was also the Bail wall, broken down and part of the surrounding ditch filled in so that the choir could be built over it. When Hugh died he was buried in this choir. So many people visited St Hugh's tomb that it was decided to build on to the choir and re-bury him in this extension under a memorial which would, it was hoped, attract even more visitors. This meant pulling down more of the city's east wall. The decision was made at a meeting of the mayor, bailiffs and other citizens with the bishop, Henry Lexington, and the dean and chapter. So the 'angel choir' was begun in 1255.

The cathedral chapter house was built between 1220 and 1235 when Robert Grosseteste was bishop. It was so-called because of the 'chapter' of the Bible which was read at the beginning of the business meetings which the bishop and canons held there.

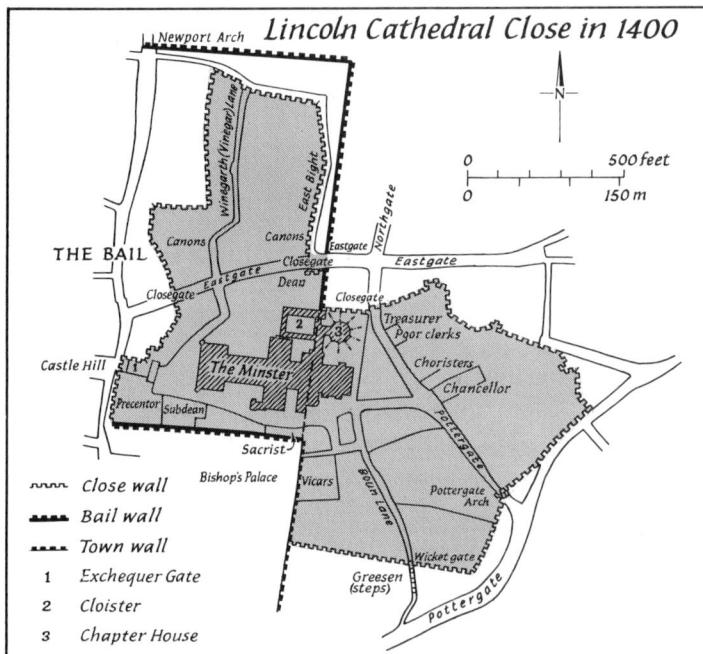

Lincoln Cathedral Close in 1400

above: *The cathedral from the north-east. At the far left is the angel choir. In front of it is the conical roof of the chapter house with its flying buttresses. The central tower was completed about 1312 and had a lofty spire which fell during a storm in 1548.*

below: *On the left you can see part of the inside of the angel choir. On the right is a detail showing one of the angels.*

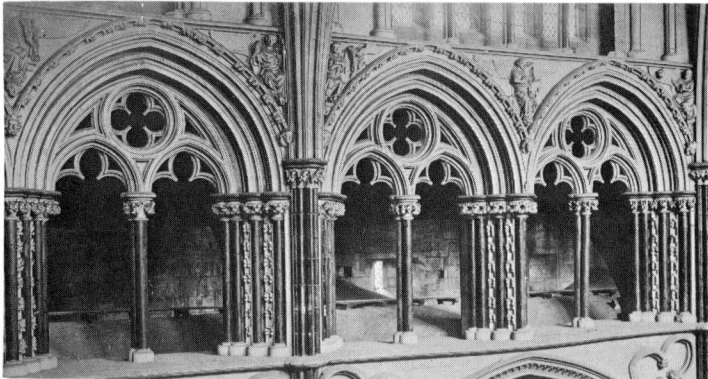

Soon after this the dean and chapter complained that they could not go from their houses to the cathedral without being attacked by citizens. So the king licensed them to build a wall 12 feet (3.6 metres) high, with turrets and gatehouses, round the cathedral. The house where the bishop lived was also being extended. In 1135, King Stephen had granted land for a bishop's house on the slope of the hill to the south of the cathedral. A great hall and kitchen had been begun in 1155. During the thirteenth century building continued. By 1327 the Bishop's Palace was probably the most splendid dwelling in Lincoln.

When the Close wall was complete the dean and chapter claimed that everyone living there need not pay the city's

right: *From the ruins of the storeroom in the Bishop's Palace you can look up to the level of the kitchen floor and the darker tiles of the fireplace.*

below: *A tower in the Close wall behind the Chancery.*

Plan of the Bishop's Palace on the level of the Hall floor

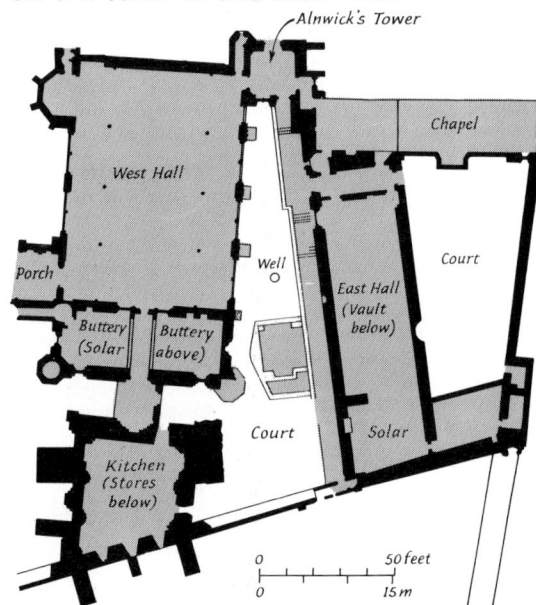

Alnwick's Tower

West Hall

Chapel

Porch

Well

Court

East Hall (Vault below)

Buttery (Solar)

Buttery above)

Court

Solar

Kitchen (Stores below)

0   50 feet
0   15 m

taxes. Also they allowed people who did not wish to be either mayor or bailiff, and who had fled into the Bail, or the Close, to escape their responsibilities. Neither the constable of the castle nor the dean and chapter would make these men return to the city and to the burden and cost of office. As early as 1275 it had been reported that the men who had been bailiffs of Lincoln could scarcely rise from poverty and misery, so great were the expenses. Yet many were eager to become freemen of Lincoln. In 1300 fifteen people had paid anything from 11d to a mark (worth 13s 4d) to be admitted freemen of Lincoln. The usual fee was half a mark.

Visitors owning animal transport would have had to rent grazing land. Therefore freemen must have made money by letting their pasture rights. By 1300 the strips of farming land held by individual freemen had been grouped into three fields, but many of the freemen had already rented their farm strips to husbandmen, who did the farming though they had no rights in respect of the pasture. When William Cause, a freeman, died in 1327, it was discovered that he held land in various places including 80 acres (about 30 hectares) in the Lincoln fields, and a windmill.

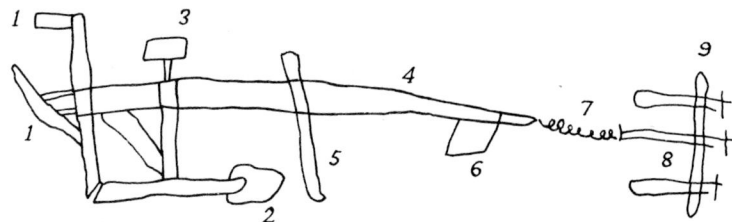

This sketch of a plough was made by a Lincolnshire accounting clerk in the thirteenth century – presumably to identify items of farm equipment that kept occurring in his lists: 1 Handles; 2 Ploughshare; 3 Mallet; 4 Plough beam; 5 Coulter; 6 Plough foot to regulate depth of ploughing; 7 Draught chain; 8 Draught pole; 9 Yoke.

below: *On the left some people are driving a cart uphill. On the right is a windmill. Both are redrawn from illustrations in the Luttrell Psalter (see note on page 2).*

Transport

Road transport was slow and unreliable. The roads were bad, sometimes impassable, and the traveller was always liable to be attacked. For example, in 1322 the chief tax collector in Lindsey reported to the royal Exchequer that they had £600 worth of taxes stored in Lincoln which they were unable to send because of the dangers of the road. When you remember that Lincoln stands at the junction of Ermine Street with the Fosse Way you will realise how dangerous some of the smaller roads must have been.

Some of Lincoln's streets must have been paved since 1301, when King Edward I had granted *pavage* (a tax to be levied on all goods brought into the city for sale). Later, the king was told that the collectors had not carried out any road work but had kept the money for themselves. And they were not the only ones at fault because in 1365 King Edward III wrote:

'It has lately come to the king's ears that by default of good rule in their city, to which merchants, alien and denizen, . . . are wont to come . . . with merchandise, such merchants on account of the deep mud and dung and filth thrown in the streets and lanes, and other loathsome things . . . come but seldom and thereby the evil name of the city . . . grows worse and worse. He, therefore, enjoins on [the citizens] to have the streets and lanes of the city cleaned at once and kept clean . . . and, if need be, compelled by grievous methods.'

It may have been safer to travel by water. The Fossdyke Canal had been built by the Romans. It linked the River

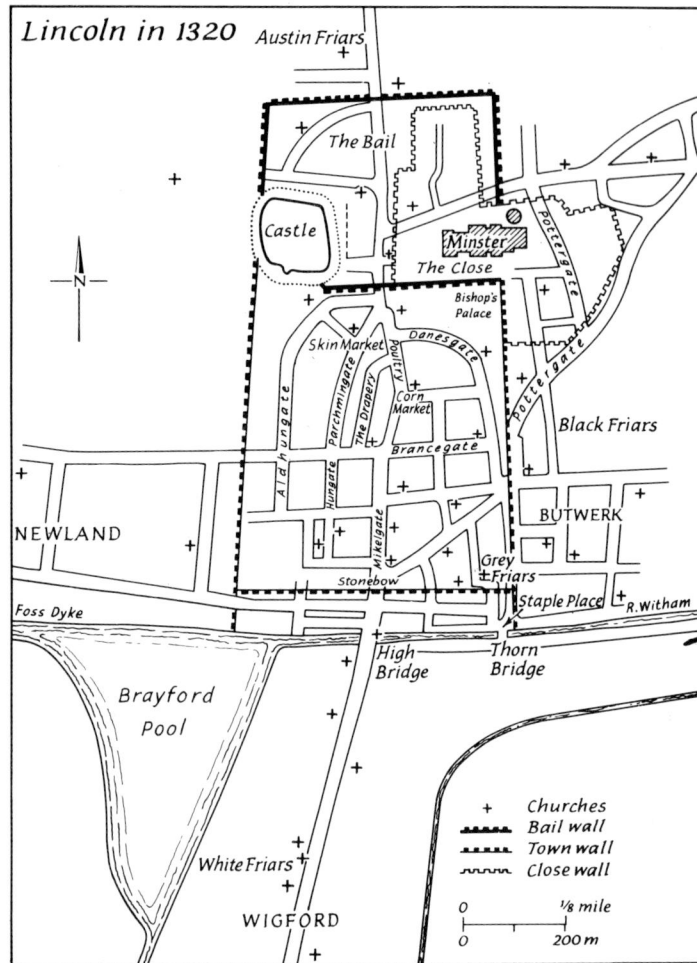

Lincoln in 1320

Austin Friars
The Bail
Castle
Minster
The Close
Pottergate
Bishop's Palace
Skin Market
Danesgate
Poultry
Corn Market
Parchmingate
The Drapery
Aldhungate
Hungate
Brancegate
Black Friars
Mikelgate
BUTWERK
NEWLAND
Grey Friars
Stonebow
Staple Place
R. Witham
Foss Dyke
High Bridge
Thorn Bridge
Brayford Pool
White Friars
WIGFORD

+ Churches
▪▪▪ Bail wall
▪▪▪ Town wall
∿∿∿ Close wall

0   ⅛ mile
0   200 m

High Bridge, Lincoln. Meat and fish were brought by river barge and sold to the townsfolk on this bridge. It was built in 1146. Houses and a chapel were later built across it.

Witham with the River Trent and the Romans used it to carry grain and wool. Now merchants used the canal to transport goods from the North Sea coast (see maps on page 6).

The seals of coastal port towns give us some idea of the kind of ship the merchants used to carry their cargoes across the North Sea. This fourteenth-century seal from Ipswich shows a ship with a square sail, stern-rudder, castles and rounded prow. Diameter 7.6 cm, 3 inches.

The wool Staple

'The Staple Place where the staple of wools, hides, woolfells and lead is held' was sited inside the south-east corner of the city wall near the River Witham, by Thornbridge, and first built in 1240. It was this 'Staple' which had made Lincoln important. The Guild Merchant had lost control of foreign trade, so in 1326 King Edward II made Lincoln one of the fourteen 'Staple' towns for wool, skins, hides, timber and tin. This meant that the city was allowed to have regular markets for the sale of these goods which could not be bought or sold anywhere in England except in a Staple town.

The setting up of the Staple (from the Old French word *estaple* – market) meant the appointment of new civic officials and the setting up of two new courts: the court of the Staple and the court of Pie Powder (*pieds poudres* or 'dusty feet'). The court of the Staple tried cases connected with the wool trade. Pie Powder tried cases that arose during the fairs. Both Lincoln and foreign merchants elected the mayor of the

below: *The Charter of 1326 setting up the wool Staple.*

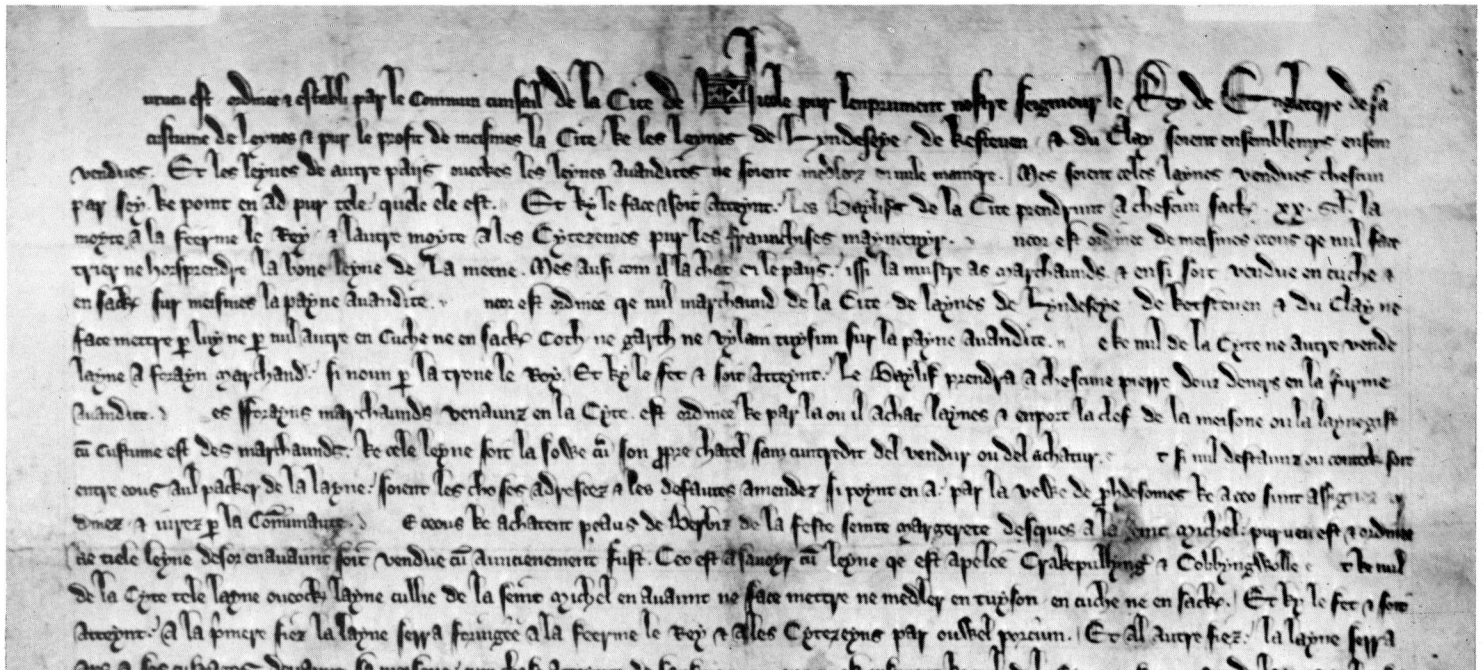

Staple, who, with the mayor of Lincoln, presided over this court, half the members of which had to be Englishmen, half foreign. William de Spaigne, a Lincoln man, was the first mayor of the Staple. The mayor of Lincoln, when presiding over Pie Powder, was helped by 'assessors', half of whom had to be foreign merchants, in those cases which occurred while a fair was being held in Lincoln and which involved a foreigner.

The new civic officials were the ponderator, chamberlains and the constables of the parishes.

The ponderator weighed all the wool brought to Lincoln and measured all the cloth made there. He did this on the 'steelyard', or weighing machine. When this weighing or measuring had been done the tax payable on the wool or cloth was assessed. When the tax had been paid the *sarplars* (bales of wool) were sealed and only then could they be sent abroad. Soon there was so much business one ponderator could no longer do it all himself, so four other freemen were chosen to be in charge of the customs, tolls and profits.

Four more freemen were elected to keep the city's accounts. Each had a key to the chest in which Lincoln's money was kept. Each parish chose two freemen to act as constables of the parish with powers to arrest people and charge them with a crime. The members of the Common Council were reduced in number to twelve and each of the twelve became a magistrate.

While foreigners came to Lincoln, Lincoln freemen went trading overseas. William Cause, for example, took 40 sacks of wool and 30 measures of lead abroad. Sometimes things went wrong; in 1323 Hugh de Tyler complained that a money-changer of St Omer in France had made off with £200 of his money. The mayor and freemen of Lincoln wrote to King Edward II on Hugh's behalf, but apparently the officials at St Omer only laughed and tore up the king's letters. So the king ordered the sheriff of London to seize the goods of the men of St Omer then living in London to the value of £200, and keep these until Hugh was satisfied.

A brass of a wool merchant, made about 1400, at the church of Stamford in Lincolnshire. He has a money purse on his belt and his feet rest on two wool-sacks or sarplars.

Markets and fairs

Although markets and fairs were essential to medieval trade, the privilege to hold either or both had to be bought and always proved expensive. Lincoln bought a charter, which cost £20, at King Edward III's first parliament in 1327. This charter increased the annual payment to the royal Exchequer from £180 to £200. But the payment soon dropped back to £180. Lincoln had, however, a chance to recoup this money because the king had confirmed the city's privilege of holding markets on Monday, Wednesday and Friday of each week. He also granted Lincoln an annual fair. The mayor, bailiffs and Common Council now had to 'keep the King's Peace'. This meant that they had to see that those people who broke the law were arrested and brought to trial. If they were found guilty and fined the money paid in fines could be added to the 'Common' purse.

Eleven years earlier the citizens had paid £300 for another royal charter. This had granted them the privileges of weighing and measuring all goods sold at the markets and fairs in the city, as well as 'the assize of bread and ale', and the resulting profits. The assize of bread and ale meant that freemen were appointed to inspect public brewhouses and bakeries, where customers could buy hot food ready for eating, or send their own food to be cooked. Prices were controlled:

The best roast pig   8d
Three roast thrushes   2d
Ten eggs   1d
For the paste, fire and trouble upon a goose   2d
(In this case customers provided their own goose to be cooked.)
The best capon baked in a pasty   8d

Bakers or brewers who exceeded these prices, gave short measure, mixed chalk or bran with bread flour, or watered the beer, were punished in the guildhall court. Brewers were licensed by the mayor and bailiffs at the standard toll of 12d a year. They could sell their ale on their premises and also by dozens to retailers, or 'tipplers', who, again could sell (or 'tip-out') half-penny or penny-worths to be consumed off the premises. Bakers paid 'baxtergeld' of either 6d or 8d. In 1331 the mayor and bailiffs were reported as trying to make money by fining offenders instead of putting them in the pillory.

'They have levied from Roger de Laghton for breach of the assize of bread and ale for a first offence 12d; from John de Sole . . . convicted a third time and deserved the pillory which punishment he redeemed for an unknown sum of money; they levied from John de Scotre, baker, for default in the assize of bread . . . a ransom of 10s. Roger de Walkeryngham, John de Parys and Emma de More, brewers, brew at their own will without any assize of their ale, for a fine to be given to the bailiffs.'

We know of another brewer in Lincoln at this time. Alice Drinkalehot brewed her own ale and got her name from the street-cry she used: 'Drink ale hot!' Alice was not one of those to be prosecuted. She had paid her tax of 10s and her business flourished.

The maintenance of the 'King's Peace' was also paid for by tolls levied on all goods offered for sale at these markets and fairs. Some of the Lincoln market tolls in 1361 were:

Every horse bought or sold   1d
Every ox   ½d
Twenty-four two-year-old sheep   1d
Each quarter of corn   1d
Each cart   2d

Shops in a medieval town. On the left is a tailor's shop; at the back are a furrier and a barber; on the right a man is selling drugs. From a fifteenth-century French manuscript.

The friars

Less splendid than the bishop's establishment, but still on a fairly large scale, were the houses of the friars. The first of these thirteenth-century religious orders to come to Lincoln were the Franciscans. They took their name from St Francis of Assisi, who lived a life of simplicity, poverty and love of living things, in an effort to recall people to the message of the Christian gospel. His followers spread all over Europe preaching and looking after the poor and the sick.

When the first friars came to Lincoln in 1231 the citizens gave them a plot of land. Building was begun and part of their friary still stands. The pictures show the timber ceiling of the upstairs chapel, the large vaulted room below (probably used as a refectory) and a drawing of the view from the south.

Other religious orders also came to Lincoln: Black Friars, White Friars and Austin Friars, but none of their houses remain. Nor do those of the older orders – Benedictines and Gilbertines – or of the other religious establishments such as the ancient leper hospital (The Malandry) or St Sepulchre's hospital near St Katherine's priory on the outskirts of the town. You can see the position of some of these buildings on the map on page 34.

Grey Friars, the house of the Franciscans in Lincoln built about 1260.

top right: *Timber ceiling.*

below right: *The undercroft.*

below: *A drawing of the building as seen from the south.*

The Black Death

Although Lincoln had become very rich between the reigns of King John and King Edward III, from this time on it steadily became poorer. The number of taxpayers had been reduced by the separation of the Bail and the Close. The city had to pay increased taxes, and, in 1349, many of its population died of the Black Death. This plague had already killed many people in western Europe. Judging from the number of wills dealt with in the burwarmot we can estimate that over half of Lincoln's population died between April and August 1349.

The bishop's registers show that in Lincoln itself 60 per cent of the clergy also died in the same period.

The deaths by plague meant fewer work-people. Goods and services became more expensive and soon everyone wanted wage increases. New national taxes, called poll taxes, were levied and soon after that, in 1381, the Peasants' Revolt broke out. The only evidence of the Peasants' Revolt in Lincoln is the letters from the Crown ordering that the rebels should be arrested and punished, and an order addressed to William Bardolph, John Bussey, William de Spaigne and others to proclaim that services and rents were to remain the same.

below: *Inscriptions carved on the wall of the tower of Ashwell church in Hertfordshire at a time when building was abandoned because of shortage of labour. At the far left you can see 'XLIX pestile[n]cia' ('49, plague). Translated from Latin the longer inscription begins '1350: wretched, wild and driven to violence the people remaining become witness at last of a tempest . . .' Such desperation must have been felt in Lincoln as in so many towns of England in these years.*

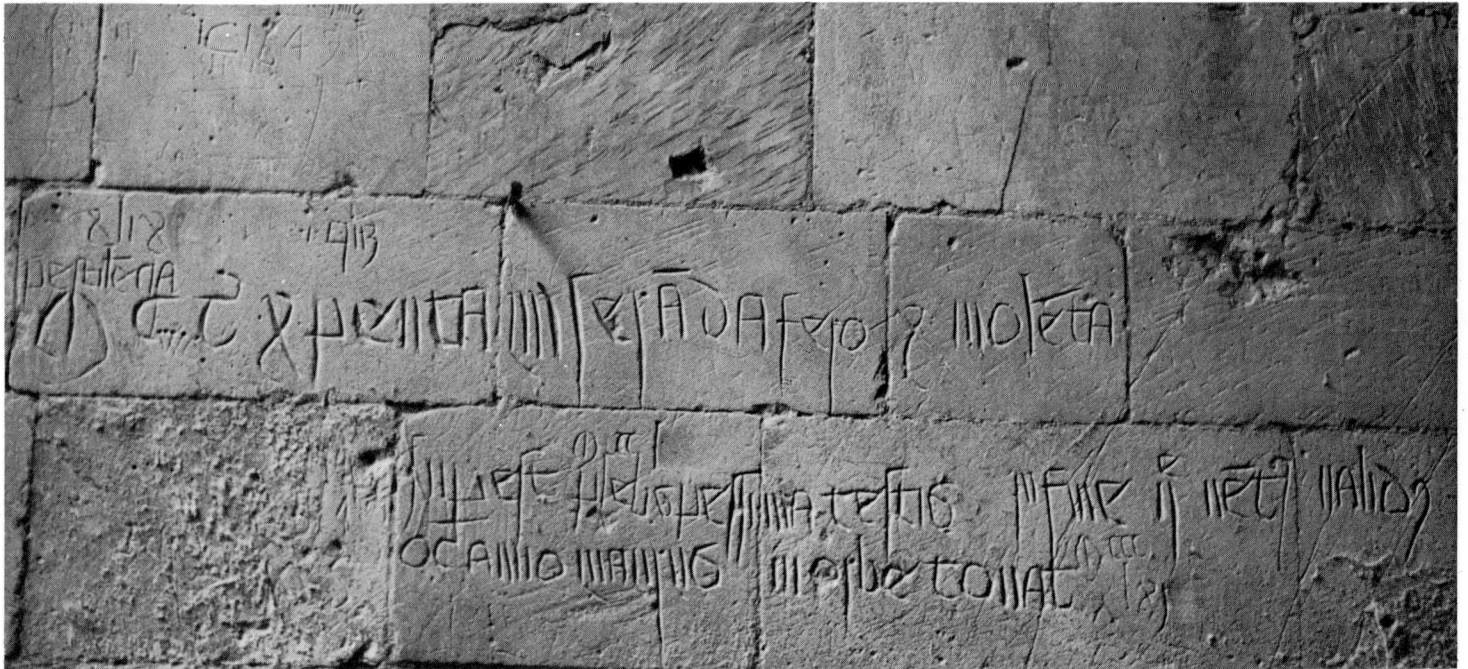

In the time of the Wars of the Roses

Edward IV arrives in Lincoln, 1461

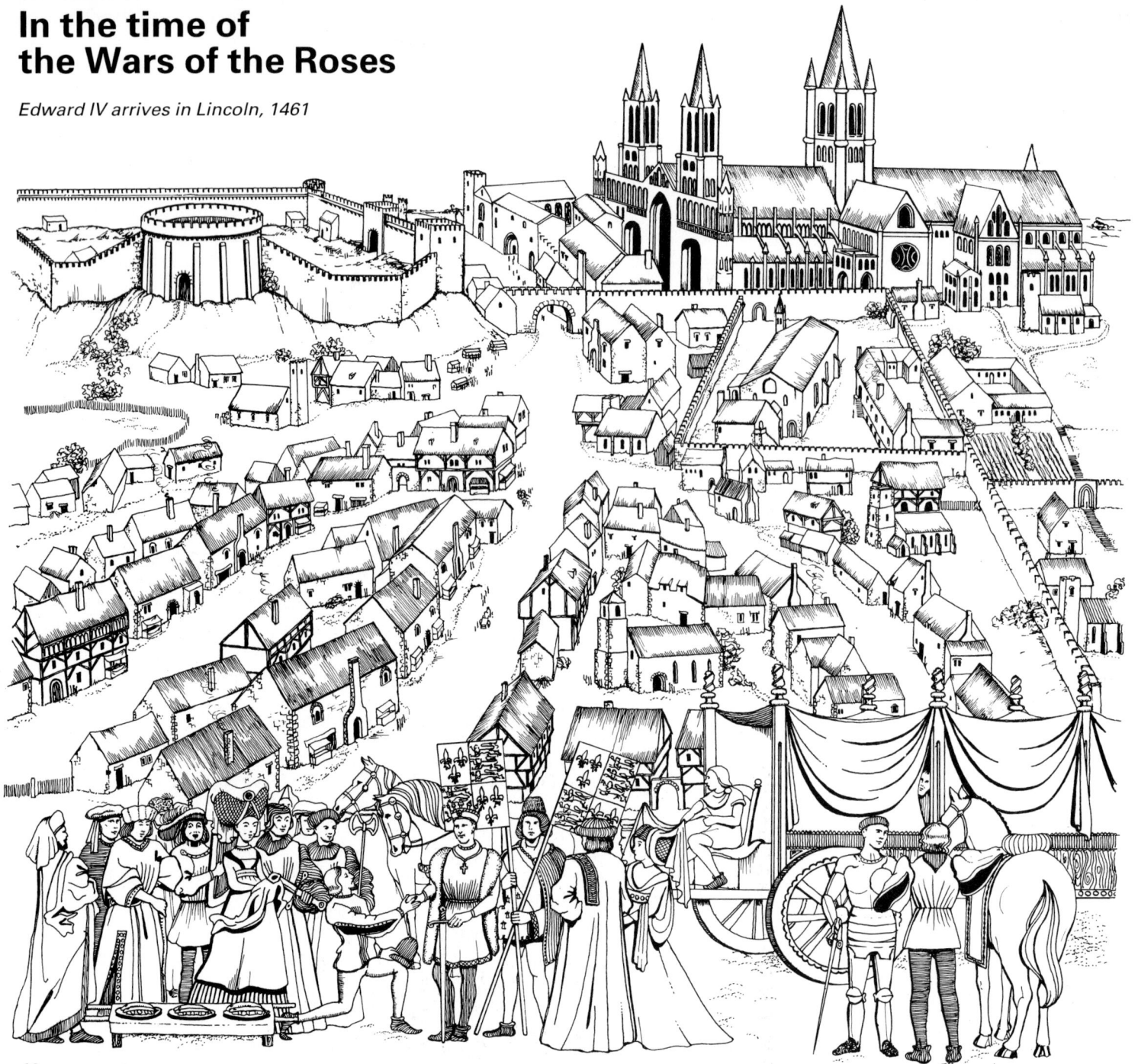

4   In the time of the Wars of the Roses

The Wars of the Roses

The mayor and corporation obviously felt that Lincoln was so poor in 1461 when King Edward IV passed through on his way to Yorkshire that all they could afford to give him was fish: twelve pike, twelve tench and twelve bream. We do not know who gave the fish to the king, for, although we know that a Guild Piscatorum (of fishermen) existed in Lincoln later, it may not have done so at this time.

Edward IV was in need of money and of political support as he was at war, in fact about to fight a battle at Towton in Yorkshire. The Wars of the Roses had begun in 1455. Edward, Duke of York had been recognised as King Edward IV by the barons of England in London in 1461. He had raised an army in London and marched north against the Lancastrians. Edward and his barons had to carry with them in carts, everything for the journey, tents for the nights when their retinue could not find a suitable house in which to sleep, beds, and the complete furnishing of Edward's private chapel. Chests contained clothes, jewels, treasures, furs, and the money with which they paid their followers and which they needed to pay for food on the journey.

Lincoln was supposed to be a Lancastrian town. It had been claimed as belonging to the dukes of Lancaster, but there is no evidence that the important people in Lincoln were unwilling to accept a Yorkist king. We must remember that the towns took little part in the Wars of the Roses.

As usual the king was met by civic officials. William Pymperton was mayor and John Elston and William Kellyngworth were the city sheriffs. There were no members of parliament because the last parliament to have been held was in 1459 at Coventry when Hamo Sutton Junior and Thomas Fitzwilliam Junior de Lincoln had represented the city. To add dignity to the occasion the mayor would have ensured that his official servants attended him, dressed in their

In 1386–7 King Richard II came to Lincoln and granted to the mayor the right to have a sword carried before him. The fourteenth-century fighting sword now kept in Lincoln guildhall was probably presented by King Richard himself.

below: *The royal arms engraved in silver gilt on the pommel of the Richard II sword.*

uniforms. They were a mace-sergeant, carrying the city's mace, the sword-bearer, carrying the sword of state, and three minstrels.

The Lincoln citizens had been allowed by the royal charter of 1409 to choose their own two sheriffs in place of the two bailiffs. These sheriffs were to be sworn in at the guildhall and were to hold their assize courts every six weeks. The old city courts were also to continue to be held regularly.

The Commonalty were also to choose the new civic officials: the four justices, of the peace, and of labourers, and artificers.

This charter of 1409 was of very great importance for Lincoln. It had been granted 'to save the city from destruction' as a result of the petition presented by the city's two members of parliament, Robert de Sutton and William de Blyton to King Henry IV in 1400.

To help Lincoln make money the charter granted the right to hold another annual fair, St Hugh's Fair, from the 2nd to the 17th of November.

Lincoln was 'so greatly devastated, reduced and diminished . . . the mayor and commonalty cannot support such . . . unless provision of aid and remedy be graciously provided'. They paid only fifty marks for this charter, which, however, dealt Lincoln an economic blow by cutting off a third of the city from taxation. It began by stating that it 'Reserved to us and our heirs dukes of Lancaster the castle of Lincoln and the ditches and walls thereof'. You remember reading on page 30 about the disputes between the mayor and bailiffs of Lincoln and Alice de Lacy and her husband, Ebulo Lestrange, which ended in the exclusion from the Bail of the city bailiffs.

This charter ended the expensive quarrel between the citizens and the dean and chapter of the cathedral. The citizens had appealed to parliament hoping to get a decision in their favour. Instead, parliament declared the Close independent of the city, and the charter states: 'We will not that the mayor, bailiffs and commonalty of Lincoln . . . have any jurisdiction . . . within the Cathedral Church of Lincoln nor the close, liberties and franchises thereof.'

The members of parliament for Lincoln were to be chosen 'in the full county court of the city, held in the guild-hall', by the mayor and about twenty-five of the more substantial citizens, 'with the consent of other worthy citizens then being present'.

This meant that the city of Lincoln was now self-governing.

The Exchequer gate, Lincoln, leads into the Close. The west front of the cathedral towers above. On the left is a sixteenth-century merchant's house.

Taxes were to be paid direct to the royal Exchequer, and not to the bailiffs as formerly. The city's officials were responsible for the keeping of the 'King's Peace'. It also meant that a few people, the freemen, would be the first to serve in these various offices and have some hope of serving without loss to themselves. This is in direct contrast to the people mentioned in the last chapter who fled into the Bail or the Close because then they were responsible for making up any losses.

It now became necessary to decide who were the Commonalty. After years of argument, in 1422, the mayor, John Sparrow, presided over a general meeting of all the reasonably well-to-do inhabitants, held in the guildhall at the special request of all the citizens. Two hundred were present. They laid down rules for the city's management. Whenever the mayor proposed anything for the good of the whole community he was to put his proposals before a committee called to a meeting in the guildhall. The members of this special committee were to be: the twelve magistrates; twenty-four of 'the more worthy men'; and forty other citizens, ten from each ward, who were to be specially nominated each year. The mayor and the twelve magistrates had the final decision. The others had the right of arguing and objecting but they had to choose a spokesman, for if anyone else of the forty dared to speak they might be fined and imprisoned at the will of the mayor and council.

The guildhall

The building of the guildhall where these committees were to meet had been begun in 1390 but had been slow because of the difficulty in raising the necessary money. In a letter to the mayor of Lincoln written in 1390 King Richard II says that he was informed that 'A hall called "The Gildehalle" situate of old time athwart the street which leads through the middle of the city, and appointed for assembly of the citizens for matters concerning the common weal, was by common consent of the citizens pulled down, because of the weakness thereof, . . . and that though by common consent and will of the commonalty another hall was begun, . . . certain citizens recking naught of honesty and advantage to the City, are refusing to contribute to the building thereof.' The king ordered the mayor to compel those citizens to pay, 'sparing not'.

In spite of the king's letter very little seems to have been done as in 1393 Sir John Bossy, the mayor of Lincoln and other people were commanded to find out what had happened to the money collected for paving city streets and building the guildhall.

above: *The city's money was kept in a chest in the guildhall. No medieval chest survives, but this one, made in 1520, is still in the Lincoln guildhall. The lid has been opened to show the complicated steel lock which was operated with several keys.*

below: *The Lincoln guildhall on the site of the south gate of the lower Roman enclosure. The upper storey is Tudor but the lower arches are fourteenth-century. The city council still meets here, summoned by the 'mote' bell which was given in 1371. It is the oldest mote bell in England.*

Hard times

Lincoln lost trade when the Fossdyke began to silt up. Many complaints were made and after each something was done, but never enough to clear the Fossdyke completely. For example, in 1365 Lincoln citizens said that they were complaining on their own behalf and also for the merchants of York, Nottingham and Kingston upon Hull. They claimed that the canal had been deliberately obstructed by farmers who had grazing land on either side of it, as well as by an unusual growth of grass and an accumulation of sand. Soon traders stopped trying to use the Fossdyke and traded at Boston instead.

This led in 1369 to the transfer of the Staple from Lincoln to Boston.

The Lincoln Commonalty seem to have defended their legal rights and privileges more stubbornly as they lost various trading advantages. And they became involved in legal wrangles which went on for years. Though tedious, these were important for the wealth of the community. One example is the quarrel between the mayor and Commonalty of Lincoln on the one hand and and the monks of St Mary's Abbey, York on the other. The problem was that once land from the city's fields had been given away or sold it was enclosed (marked off from the rest of Lincoln's fields) and its new owners paid nothing towards the city's taxes; not even the penny landgable. This was serious because the freemen lost a great deal of money in this way.

The quarrel began because a freemen named Romfarus in 1115 had given a burgage tenement and its strips to St Mary's Abbey, York. The monks had gradually added other gifts and had bought some of the other burgage tenements, so that, by 1455, they had acquired nearly 300 acres (120 hectares). From 1392 no monk lived on this land which was, by then, let to laymen, and pigs were kept in the west end of their chapel. The quarrel ended in 1455 when the monks gave up their land in Bagerholm Wong and St Hugh's Croft and four houses in St Mark's parish, and enclosed the rest. The mayor and Commonalty and the monks agreed on various rights of way. One from Monks' Road to the Lindum Terrace has been a right of way ever since. The monks granted the city the Blackdyke Ditch to load the ships and boats. The city granted the monks free passage in and out of Blackdyke, but only the mayor could allow them to fish or go wildfowling in the Blackdyke.

Lincoln Common Council decided who became freemen. The freedom of the city could be inherited by a son but not by a daughter. It was no longer possible to become a freeman simply by living in Lincoln for a year and a day and then getting one's name on the official list. Now, to try and persuade rich and important people to come and live there and share in the payment of taxes, the freedom of Lincoln could be given as a gift, or sold to the highest bidder. Finally, anyone who had served a seven-year apprenticeship to a freeman became a freeman himself if he applied to the Council. This was a change from the rules in the reign of King John when somebody already a member of a craft guild who wished to become a freeman had to renounce his craft and get rid of the tools of his trade before he could do so. Now he could continue as a craftsman and become a freeman.

The Stint, or restriction on the number of animals that might be grazed freely on the common pasture, was strongly enforced at this time because some freemen were going in for stock breeding, particularly beef cattle. The number of public windmills was increased and anyone who grew grain on the city's lands was obliged to have that grain ground in the public mills and to pay heavily for the privilege.

Some freemen seem to have thought that their children would have better chances of employment if they had grammar school education. The number of boys attending the school which had been sited in the lower town since 1461, increased considerably during the fifteenth century.

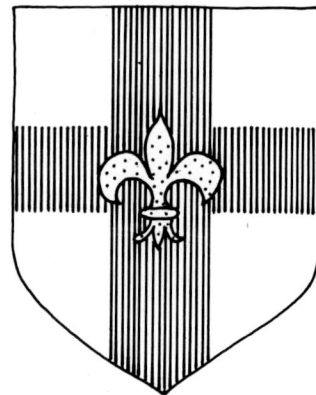

The arms of the city of Lincoln are a silver background with a golden lily on a red cross. The lily represents the Virgin Mary, patron saint of the city and the cathedral. These arms appear on a seal of 1449. It is reproduced by permission of the mayor and corporation.

Town houses

Ground space within the city walls was valuable because it was scarce. As their families grew, or as they had more apprentices and servants, the rich in Lincoln built upwards. Some of the buildings of this kind that survive (though much restored) such as 'The Cardinal's Hat' and 'The Green Dragon', are three storeys tall. They are of half-timbered construction like the one shown here. Many houses now had flues and chimneys. The flues led into chimney stacks made either of stone or of brick. This type of house often had the ground floor walls built of stone to carry the weight of the upper floors.

The stairs, which were of oak planks, were now inside the houses. The living room was still on the first floor and it was lit by a series of small, glazed windows set in the long wall which overhung the ground floor and the street. The second floor

'The Green Dragon', once a wool merchant's house by the river near the Thornbridge. The earliest construction is fourteenth-century but later alterations have been made.

overhung the first and was also lit by smaller glazed windows. This overhang made the space between the facing houses very narrow, although at street level, on wider streets, there were from 4.5 to 6 metres between facing houses. The main rooms would have had their walls panelled with vertical boards painted, either in the fashionable colours of green and gold, or with historical or biblical scenes. Sometimes the walls were still hung with cloths; instead of being painted the picture was stitched onto or woven into the fabric itself as a tapestry. To lessen the draught the table where the head of the house dined was placed on a dais, or platform, and given a backing of fabric. Over the chair where the head of the household sat was a canopy emblazoned with a 'cloth of estate'. By 1461 tapestry was the rule for hall and chamber.

The furniture was much as it had been. Most of the rich families would now have a sideboard, or 'cupboard', on which to show off the pewter, silver or gold cups, and platters they owned. They might also have an 'almery' (what we now call a cupboard), where they kept books, charters and documents.

We do not know whether King Edward IV got any money

opposite: *The chancellor of Lincoln cathedral lived in a large house in the Close. The pictures show a fifteenth-century wing of the house, and a doorway.*

above: *The 'squint', a tiny pair of windows let into the bedroom wall to give a view into the chapel'.*

right: *The chapel screen.*

below: *Between two doors of a private dining hall in the Bishop's Palace is a 'sideboard' beneath a carved canopy.*

from Lincoln at this time or not. Yet he obviously felt kindly towards the city because in 1462, after he had been crowned in London, he wrote to the mayor and citizens of Lincoln and excused them from paying £100 of the £180 the city owed to the royal Exchequer each year. Further, in an attempt to increase the number of taxable inhabitants in the county of the city of Lincoln, he granted in 1466: 'On account of the desolation and decay of the city, and the ruin of houses, and the poverty and fewness of the inhabitants, to the mayor, sheriffs and commonalty and their successors for ever that the townships and towns of Branston, Waddington, Bracebridge and Canwick should become part of the county of the city of Lincoln'.

Yet, in spite of setbacks, in four centuries Lincoln had grown into something very different from the wooden huddle of 1069.